s/o H/1

✔ KT-403-531

NAPIER COLLEGE LIBRARY
SIGHTHILL
Sighthill Court
Edinburgh EH11 4BN
Tel 031-443 6061
Ext 307

This book is due for return on or before
the last date stamped below

16 MAY 1985

Accn no.	83 092781	01

PRENTICE-HALL FOUNDATIONS OF FINANCE SERIES

PRENTICE-HALL FOUNDATIONS OF FINANCE SERIES

Ezra Solomon, *Editor*

The Lease Versus Buy Decision

Harold Bierman, Jr.

Cornell University

PRENTICE-HALL, INC., Englewood Cliffs, New Jersey 07632

Library of Congress Cataloging in Publication Data

Bierman, Harold. (date)
    The lease versus buy decision.

    (Prentice-Hall foundation of finance series)
    Bibliography: p. 107
    Includes index.
    1. Industrial equipment leases. I. Title. II. Series.
HD39.4.B53   658.1'5242   81-23512
ISBN 0-13-527994-1   AACR2
ISBN 0-13-527986-0 (pbk.)

Editorial/production supervision: Richard C. Laveglia
Manufacturing buyer: Ed O'Dougherty

© 1982 by Prentice-Hall, Inc., Englewood Cliffs, N.J. 07632

*All rights reserved. No part of this book
may be reproduced in any form or
by any means without permission in writing
from the publisher.*

Printed in the United States of America

10   9   8   7   6   5   4   3   2   1

ISBN 0-13-527994-1
ISBN 0-13-527986-0 pbk

Prentice-Hall International, Inc., *London*
Prentice-Hall of Australia Pty. Limited, *Sydney*
Prentice-Hall of Canada, Ltd., *Toronto*
Prentice-Hall of India Private Limited, *New Delhi*
Prentice-Hall of Japan, Inc., *Tokyo*
Prentice-Hall of Southeast Asia Pte. Ltd., *Singapore*
Whitehall Books Limited, *Wellington, New Zealand*

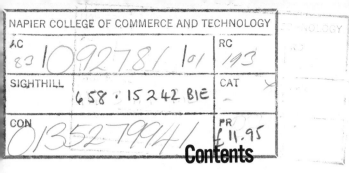

NAPIER COLLEGE OF COMMERCE AND TECHNOLOGY

AC 83 | 092781 | 01 | RC 193

SIGHTHILL 658.15242 BIE | CAT

CON 0135279941 | PR £11.95

Contents

VII   Pros and Cons of Leasing   92

VIII   The Economic Recovery Tax Act of 1981   102

Selected References   107

Index   109

Editor's Note

The subject matter of financial management is in the process of rapid change. A growing analytical content, virtually nonexistent ten years ago, has displaced the earlier descriptive treatment as the center of emphasis in the field.

These developments have created problems for both teachers and students. On the one hand, recent and current thinking, which is addressed to basic questions that cut across traditional divisions of the subject matter, do not fit neatly into the older structure of academic courses and texts in corporate finance. On the other hand, the new developments have not yet stabilized and as a result have not yet reached the degree of certainty, lucidity, and freedom from controversy that would permit all of them to be captured within a single, straightforward treatment at the textbook level. Indeed, given the present rate of change, it will be years before such a development can be expected.

One solution to the problem, which the present Foundations of Finance Series tries to provide, is to cover the major components of the subject through short independent studies. These individual essays provide a vehicle through which the writer can concentrate on a single sequence of ideas and thus communicate some of the excitement of current thinking and controversy. For the teacher and student, the separate self-contained books provide a flexible up-to-date survey of current thinking on each subarea covered and at the same time permit maximum flexiblity in course and curriculum design.

EZRA SOLOMON

Preface

The leasing of assets is common practice. As individuals we engage in leasing of a sort when we rent a car at the airport, rent an apartment to live in for a year, or reserve a hotel room for a night.

For different reasons it was decided to buy the use of the asset for a well-defined period of time and to pay a contractual amount rather than to buy the asset. The motivation for leasing the car at the airport and hotel room was that the use was going to be of short duration and that it made good economic sense to lease rather than to incur the transaction costs of buying and selling the asset. The decision to rent the apartment for a year was less obviously a desirable decision as compared with buying.

Corporations have analogous decisions with added complexities. The tax deductions, accounting measures, risk conditions, and economic consequences will differ depending on whether the asset is purchased or leased.

Our objective in this book is to develop techniques for analyzing the decision to buy or lease an asset. We should be able to convince you that there are some obvious errors that you can avoid. We shall also suggest some reasonable methods of analyzing the decision.

A lease decision combines the elements of making an investment and the elements of borrowing money. Because of the dual factors involved in determining whether to lease or to buy, the buy-lease decision is more complex than a normal investment decision or a financing decision. An effort will be made to minimize complexity, but a certain amount of complexity still will remain. Only patience and high school algebra will be required to understand the problem and its solution.

One warning is appropriate for the decision maker in this area. Lessors are likely to be interested in having a lease contract signed; thus any analysis prepared by a person with an economic interest in the lease should be reviewed with care.

Many people were indispensible in aiding me to develop this book. I am especially indebted to Professors Richard S. Bower of Dartmouth College, Ned C. Hill of Indiana University, and David H. Downes of the University of California for their reviews of the original manuscript and their constructive criticisms.

Harold Bierman, Jr.

111111111111111111111111111111111111111111111111111111111111111111111111111111111
111111111111111111111111111111111111111111111111111111111111111111111111111111111
1111111111111111111111111111111111111111   111111111111111111111111111111111111111
1111111111111111111111111111111111111111   111111111111111111111111111111111111111
1111111111111111111111111111111111111111   111111111111111111111111111111111111111
1111111111111111111111111111111111111111   111111111111111111111111111111111111111
1111111111111111111111111111111111111111   111111111111111111111111111111111111111
1111111111111111111111111111111111111111   111111111111111111111111111111111111111
1111111111111111111111111111111111111111   111111111111111111111111111111111111111
1111111111111111111111111111111111111111   111111111111111111111111111111111111111
1111111111111111111111111111111111111111   111111111111111111111111111111111111111
1111111111111111111111111111111111111111   111111111111111111111111111111111111111
111111111111111111111111111111111111111111111111111111111111111111111111111111111
111111111111111111111111111111111111111111111111111111111111111111111111111111111

The Basic Lease Analysis

PICK up an annual report of a major corporation and inspect the footnotes. There is likely to be a footnote describing leases that the company has contracted. It would be a rare corporation that had zero leases.

Leasing is jointly a method of financing and a method of acquiring an asset. Practically any item that can be leased can also be bought; thus there is a decision to be made as to whether to buy or lease. The objective of this book is to suggest an approach to evaluating the economic costs of buying as compared with leasing. Unfortunately it is easier to describe errors that are likely to be made than to recommend a simple universally accepted method of analysis.

Three Basic Problems

There are three basic problems in analyzing buy versus lease decisions. One is the definition of the cash flows to be used. The second is the choice of the rate of discount. The third problem is to match the appropriate rate of discount with the choice of cash flow.

We shall generally recommend the use of after-tax cash flows. For purposes of simplification, a zero tax rate will sometimes be used so that the before-tax and after-tax cash flows are identical.

A major problem with the cash flow calculation is the inclusion or exclusion of the debt component of the lease flows. The objective is to make the lease analysis comparable in terms of debt characteristics with the buy analysis. Generally this means extracting elements of the lease cash flows.

There are three basic choices for the rate of discount to be used:

1. the after-tax borrowing rate
2. the before-tax borrowing rate
3. some type of risk-adjusted rate such as the weighted average cost of capital

If we assume that there are four possible sets of cash flows (there are more) and three possible discount rates (again, there are more), there are then twelve different ways of combining the two elements. If we then recognize the possibility of using different rates of discount to discount different types of cash flows for either the buy or the lease component, we can readily see why there has not been agreement on analyzing buy versus lease decisions.

Finally, there is the matter of comparing the cash flows of one alternative (buy) with the other alternative (lease). Rather than reviewing the basic theory and practice of capital budgeting, we shall jump into the middle of that discussion and conclude that one should use the net present value method since it is at least as good as any other method and, for many purposes, better.[1]

The Net Present Value Method

The alternatives will be evaluated using the net present value method. Future cash flows will be transferred back to the present moment in time using present value factors. Each present value factor is equal to $(1 + r)^{-n}$, where r is the discount rate being used and n is the number of time periods in the future when the cash is to be received. Multiplying the future cash flow by $(1 + r)^{-n}$, gives a present value equivalent. The sum of these present value equivalents gives the net present value of the alternative.

For example, if $100 is to be paid at time 2 and if the interest rate is .10, we have

$$(1 + r)^{-2} = (1.10)^{-2} = .826446$$

The present value factor is .826446 and the present value equivalent of the $100 to be paid at time 2 is $82.64.

---

[1]The reader not accepting this statement might read H. Bierman, Jr., and S. Smidt, *The Capital Budgeting Decision*, 5th ed. (New York: Macmillan, 1980).

An investment is acceptable if its net present value is equal to or larger than zero. For example, assume a firm has a .10 time value factor and the cash flows of an investment are as follows:

Time	Cash Flows
0	-18,000
1	11,000
2	12,100

We want to compute the net present value of the investment by multiplying each cash flow by $(1.10)^{-n}$, where n represents the time the cash flow takes place. We now have

Time: n	Cash Flows	Present Value Factors	Present Values
0	-18,000	$(1.10)^{-0}$	-18,000
1	11,000	$(1.10)^{-1}$	10,000
2	12,100	$(1.10)^{-2}$	10,000
		Net present value	2,000

The net present value of the investment is positive; thus the investment is acceptable.

If mutually exclusive investments are being compared, and if, because of their nature, only one investment can be accepted (they can be different ways of doing the same tasks), the investment with the largest net present value would be chosen as the best alternative.

The explanations just presented are excessively brief and they omit many complexities. But these complexities would not alter the basic calculations or the two basic decision rules. Accept an investment if its net present value is positive. Choose the mutually exclusive investment with the largest net present value.

We will now consider the basic problem of choosing between leasing and buying.

The Basic Problem

In this chapter we assume zero taxes so that we can concentrate on the basic elements of the buy versus lease decision. We also assume that there is no uncertainty. In the example following we know that the equipment is to be acquired, that the life is three years, and that there is no residual value. The cost of the equipment if purchased is $90,000, and it can be leased for $36,829 with the lease payments being made at the end of each of the next three years. Capital can be borrowed at the bank at an interest cost of .10. The repayment schedule is flexible. The lease is not cancellable by the lessee.

Should the equipment be bought or leased? Since it has already been decided that the equipment should be acquired, the only question is as to the method of financing. While the problem has been described as a buy versus lease decision, actually it is a method of financing decision.

The firm has the following capital structure with a weighted average cost of capital of .14.

Method of Financing	Cost	Capital Structure Weights	Weighted Cost
Debt	.10	.5	.05
Equity	.18	.5	.09
		Weighted average cost of capital	.14

The present value of the lease payments using .14 as the discount rate is $85,504.

Time	Lease Payment	Present Value Factors	Present Values
1	36,829	1.14^{-1}	32,306
2	36,829	1.14^{-2}	28,339
3	36,829	1.14^{-3}	24,859
		Present value of leasing	85,504

The cost of buying is $90,000 and the present value of leasing is only $85,504; thus leasing would seem to be more desirable than buying.

We have just illustrated a major error in buy versus lease analysis. One has to be very careful about the cash flows that are being used and the rates of discount. The above calculations are not correct.

Let us assume that the analyst is a naïve but intelligent person who does not understand present value analysis. Instead of doing the calculations, the analyst phones the bank lending officer and asks one question: "How much will the corporation have to pay at the end of each time period to repay a loan of $90,000?" The .10 interest rate and the three-year time period have already been defined. The bank lending officer makes a relatively simple calculation and responds that the required annual payments are $36,190 at the end of each of three years. With that payment schedule the bank will earn a .10 return each year and the company will pay interest at the rate of .10 per year.

Now the analyst has the choice of recommending the buying of the equipment and paying the bank $36,190 each year or leasing and paying the lessor $36,829. With the choice described in this manner, the preference for buying in this situation becomes obvious. The firm would rather write three checks to the bank for $36,190 than write three checks of $36,829 to the lessor.

The present value calculation led to an incorrect decision since the choice of the rate of discount was wrong. If .10 (the borrowing rate) had been used, we would have obtained $91,588 for the present value of leasing.

Time	Lease Payment	Present Value Factors	Present Values
1	36,829	1.10^{-1}	33,481
2	36,829	1.10^{-2}	30,437
3	36,829	1.10^{-3}	27,670
		Present value of leasing	91,588

Now leasing has a larger present value of costs ($91,588) than does buying ($90,000). Again, buying is more desirable than leasing.

The Two Correct Methods

Two correct methods of analysis have been presented. One is to determine the cash outlay per period for buying combined with borrowing as compared with leasing. Note that the buy analysis was combined with the borrowing necessary to finance the asset so that buying could be compared with leasing, which is an alternative type of debt. In a real sense we are comparing two different types of financing.

The second method of analysis computed the present value of the lease payments and compared the present value of leasing with the cost of the asset. The cost of debt was used to compute the present value. The use of the weighted average cost of capital led to an incorrect decision. It caused leasing to appear to be less costly than buying when in fact it was more costly. The inclusion of a risk adjustment in the discount rate led to an incorrect observation.

Residual Value

In the example presented, buying was more desirable than leasing despite the fact that the residual value of the equipment was equal to zero. Now we will change the assumptions. The lease payments are now reduced to $36,000 per year. With zero residual value, leasing is now more desirable than buying. But now assume that the residual value at time 3 is $1,500. How should this information be incorporated into the analysis? There are several possible approaches, but only one will be suggested here. First, compute the present value of the lease payments using the .10 borrowing rate. This is $89,527. Then, subtract the present value of the residual value from the cost of the equipment. Using .14 as the discount rate, we would have

$$\text{Net cost of buying} = 90,000 - 1,500(1.14)^{-3} = 90,000 - 1,500(.6750) = 88,987$$

and buying is more desirable than leasing. But someone could object to the use of the .14 rate of discount, so we must relax that assumption. Figure 1.1 shows the net cost of buying and the cost of leasing for different discount rates. The cost of buying (net of residual value) is equal to the cost of leasing if the residual value is equal to $1,500 and if the residual value is discounted at a discount rate of .47.[2]

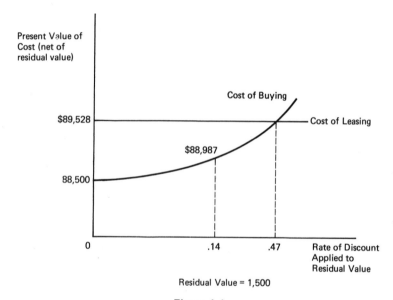

Figure 1.1

Note that the cost of leasing is not affected by the use of different rates of discount being used for the cost of buying. The cost of leasing has been computed using the borrowing rate defined to be .10. That number is not being

---

[2] The calculation of .47 is as follows:

$$90,000 - 1,500(1 + r)^{-3} = 89,528$$
$$(1 + r)^{-3} = .3147$$
$$r = .47$$

allowed to change. The rate at which the residual value should be discounted is being varied. We find that buying is preferred to leasing over a wide range of discount rates (as long as the discount rate is less than .47).

The Investment Decision

Let us return to the situation in which there is zero residual value and the lease payment is $36,829 per period. The weighted average cost of capital is again .14.

Method of Financing	Cost	Capital Structure Weights	Weighted Cost
Debt	.10	.5	.05
Equity	.18	.5	.09

Weighted average cost of capital   .14

If the benefits each year are forecasted to be $38,000, what should the firm do? We assume that the decision to acquire the asset has not yet been made.

A straightforward capital budgeting analysis using the .14 weighted average cost of capital indicates that the investment has a negative net present value of $1,778 and should be rejected.

Time	Cash Flow	Present Value Factors	Present Values
0	-90,000	1.14^{-0}	-90,000
1	38,000	1.14^{-1}	33,333
2	38,000	1.14^{-2}	29,240
3	38,000	1.14^{-3}	25,649

Net present value   -1,778

Shifting to the consideration of leasing where the lease payment is $36,829 per year, we see that each year has a positive cash flow of $1,171: $38,000 – $36,829 = $1,171. The present value of leasing is positive using any interest rate.

It would seem that the firm should lease, but this conclusion is in error. It has already been shown that with these facts buying is more desirable than leasing.

In the calculations using .14 as the discount rate we obtain a present value of benefits $88,222. The present value of leasing (using .10) has already been computed to be $91,588. Thus if .14 were to be accepted as the appropriate rate for discounting benefits and .10 as the rate of discounting the lease flows, leasing, as well as buying, would have to be rejected.

If the leasing alternative were to be accepted, then we should reconsider (and restructure) the buy decision. Using $90,000 of debt we know that the debt payments each year will be $36,190. The net benefits of buying each year are $38,000 - $36,190 = $1,810, a figure that exceeds the yearly $1,171 net benefits of leasing.

Using .10 leasing has a present value of costs $91,588, which is larger than the $90,000 cost of buying. A method of analysis that indicates that leasing is acceptable but buying is not, given the facts of this example, must be deficient.

Comparing the annual $38,000 benefit with the $36,829 lease payment is analogous to subtracting the debt payment of $36,190 from the benefit if the asset is purchased. One cannot include the debt payments of leasing in the cash flows, without including the debt payments in the buy analysis. A second alternative is to exclude the debt payments from both alternatives. The buy and lease alternatives must be made comparable relative to the inclusion or exclusion of the debt flows.

Should the equipment be acquired? The lease analysis clearly shows that, if $38,000 of benefits is certain with lease payments of $36,829, this is a good alternative. The buy analysis makes the point more forcefully since the debt payments are less with buying than with leasing.

However, if the benefit stream is not certain, it is no longer obvious that buying (or leasing) is acceptable. Should the equipment be acquired? It depends on the risk analysis. Thus we will stop short of declaring that the acquisition is desirable. What we can say is that, if the equipment is acquired, with the facts as given, the equipment should be bought not leased. We need a method of analysis that will lead to sensible decisions.

We are assuming that the necessary funds can be borrowed at a cost of .10. We are also assuming, for simplicity, that the debt will be repaid in equal installments. This latter assumption is not necessary for the basic analysis but is used to illustrate the fact that buying is clearly superior in the present situation.

We have been comparing leasing with a buy alternative in which the financing is being accomplished using borrowed funds. Having decided that buy and borrow is better than leasing, the firm might then decide that the use of common stock is even better than borrowing the funds. We have definitely not proven that debt is more desirable than common stock. It has been shown that straight borrowing is more desirable than leasing with the given facts.

If with the given facts a firm concluded that the common stock were more desirable than straight debt, but that leasing were more desirable than common stock, this would be upsetting. Transitivity of choice must apply here. If debt is less costly than leasing and if common stock is less costly than debt, then it is not possible to conclude that leasing is less costly than common stock.

The Next Step

We have presented a relatively simple method of choosing between buying and leasing. However, we have assumed an artificial situation of zero taxes. The next step is to review in the next chapter the buy versus lease decision assuming the existence of corporate income taxes.

Conclusions

This chapter has introduced two of the primary complexities of buy versus lease analysis: the computation of the cash flows and the choice of the rate of discount. With cash flows, the lesson to be learned is that buying and leasing must be placed on a comparable basis. With the rate of discount, one has to be careful using a risk-adjusted rate of discount for some of the cash flows but not for others. The choice of the rate of discount is not separable from the calculation of cash flows problem.

It is interesting that a high level of complexity can be introduced even when the tax rate is assumed to be zero. Taxes add their own complexity.

Appendix I

Let

$$V_B = \text{the net cost of buying}$$
$$V_L = \text{the net cost of leasing}$$
$$L = \text{the annual lease payment}$$
$$k_i = \text{the cost of debt}$$
$$C = \text{the cost (initial outlay) of investment}$$
$$R_n = \text{the residual value at time } n$$
$$n = \text{the life of the investment}$$
$$B(n, k_i) = \text{the present value of an annuity for } n \text{ periods and } k_i \text{ interest rate}$$
$$k = \text{any rate of discount}$$

The net cost of buying is

$$V_B = C - R_n (1 + k)^{-n}$$

The net cost of leasing is

$$V_L = L [B(n, k_i)]$$

Exercises

1. The A Company has decided to acquire a piece of equipment but has not yet decided to buy or lease. The lease payments would be $140,105 paid annually at the end of each year. If purchased at a cost of $400,000, the equipment would be financed with debt costing .10, which can be repaid at any time within the four-year period. The life of the equipment is four years. The lease is a firm commitment to make four payments. There is no salvage value. Should the firm lease or buy-borrow? There are no taxes.

2. (Continuation of Exercise 1) Assume that the firm has not yet decided to purchase (or lease) the equipment. The benefits (known with certainty) are $145,000 per year. The firm has a normal hurdle rate of .20. There are no taxes. The firm will use .10 debt if the asset is purchased. Should the firm buy or lease? Should it do nothing? The firm can still lease at $140,105 per year.

3. Assume zero taxes. Equipment can be leased at $10,000 per year (first payment one year hence) for ten years or purchased at a cost of $64,177. The company has a weighted average cost of capital of 15 percent. A bank has indicated that it would be willing to make a loan of $64,177 at a cost of 10 percent. Should the company buy or lease?
   There are no uncertaintities. The equipment will be used for ten years. There is zero salvage value.

4. (Continuation of Exercise 3) If the bank were willing to lend funds at 9 percent, should the company buy or lease?

5. (Continuation of Exercise 3) If the company pays $64,177 for the equipment, it will save $10,000 a year in lease payments for ten years. What rate of return will it earn on its "investment"?

6. A firm can borrow $10,000 for two years at a cost per year of .10. No debt payments are to be made until time 2. There are zero taxes.
   a. What is the net present value of all the debt flows if .10 is used to discount the cash flows?
   b. What if .20 is used?
   c. What if .05 is used?

7. A firm can borrow $10,000 for two years at a cost per year of .10. How does the net present value of the debt flows affect the net present value of the investment?

8. An asset costs $1,000,000 and is expected to have residual value of $150,000 in 20 years. The firm uses a .10 discount rate. What is the cost, net of residual value, of buying the asset?

9. (Reference Exercise 3)
   a. What does the residual value have to be at time 10 for the firm to be indifferent to buying and leasing? Assume that the firm wants to use .15 as the time value factor to discount any residual value.
   b. How does the answer change if .10 is used as the discount rate?

10. a. If an investment earning $11,000 per year can be financed with debt requiring outlays of $10,000 per year over the same time period, should it be acquired?
    b. Should the investment be acquired if it can be leased?

11. Assume zero taxes. Equipment can be leased at $10,000 per year (first payment one year hence) for ten years or purchased at a cost of $56,502. The company has a weighted average cost of capital of 15 percent. The equipment will have zero salvage value. A bank has indicated that it would be willing to make the loan (equal payment) of $56,502 at a cost of 10 percent.
a. Should the company buy or lease?
b. Is your answer to part a subject to an assumption? Explain.

Solutions

1. Equal debt payments would result in payments of $126,187 compared with $140,105 if leased; therefore borrow and buy:

$$\frac{400,000}{3.1699} = 126,187$$

where

$$B(4, .10) = 3.1699.$$

2. $B(4, .20) = 2.5887$,

$$145,000 \times 2.5877 = 375,362$$

and

$$NPV = -400,000 + 375.362 = 24,638 \text{ (using .20)}$$

The present value of the $145,000 benefits using .20 is $375,362. The cost is $400,000. Thus using .20 as the discount rate, the decision would be to reject. However, the benefits are $145,000 and the lease cost is $140,105, both known with certainty; therefore leasing is desirable. A hurdle rate of .20 is not appropriate if the benefits are certain.

But Exercise 1 concluded that, if the equipment was acceptable, we should buy and borrow. The difficulty is that the lease decision analysis includes the debt flows (leases) in the cash flow. We can also include the debt flow ($126,187) in the buy alternative, and buy-borrow would again be better than leasing.

If risk is acknowledged, then the investment opportunity may be rejected. However, the buy-borrow analysis and the lease should be on the same basis. If the debt flows are included in leasing, they should also be included in buy-borrow. The analyses must be comparable. Normally the debt increases risk; in this example, with the cash flows known with certainty, risk is decreased with more debt.

3. Bank payments are $64,177/6.1446 = $10,444. Since $10,444 > $10,000, lease.

4. Indifference, because $64,177/6.4177 = $10,000. Note that the 15 percent weighted average cost of capital is not used.

5. 9 percent.

6. a. $NPV = 0$.
   b. $NPV = \$10,000 - (\$12,100/1.20^2) = \$1,597$.
   c. $NPV = \$10,000 - (\$12,100/1.05^2) = -\$975$.
7. The net present values as well as the cash flows are excluded from the investment analysis.
8. The present value of residual value $= \$150,000(1.10)^{-20} = \$22,297$; net cost $= \$1,000,000 - \$22,297 = \$997,703$.
9. a. $64,177 - (1.15)^{-10}R = 10,000\ B(10, .10)$
$$64,177 - .2472R = 61,446$$
$$.2472R = 2,731$$
$$R = 11,048$$
   b.
$$(1.10)^{-10}R = 2,731$$
$$.3855R = 2,731$$
$$R = 7,084$$
10. a. Depends on risk. Are the $11,000 per year of earnings certain?
    b. Same answer.
11. a. Because $\$56,502/6.1446 = \$9,195$, which is less than $10,000, buy-borrow is better than lease.
    b. No assumptions other than those in the problem. The choice assumes only that the banker can do arithmetic or will let you do it for him or her.

```
2222222222222222222222222222222222222222222222222222222222222222222222222222222222
2222222222222222222222222222222222222222222222222222222222222222222222222222222222
2222222222222222222222222222222222222222   222   2222222222222222222222222222222222
2222222222222222222222222222222222222222   222   2222222222222222222222222222222222
2222222222222222222222222222222222222222   222   2222222222222222222222222222222222
2222222222222222222222222222222222222222   222   2222222222222222222222222222222222
2222222222222222222222222222222222222222   222   2222222222222222222222222222222222
2222222222222222222222222222222222222222   222   2222222222222222222222222222222222
2222222222222222222222222222222222222222   222   2222222222222222222222222222222222
2222222222222222222222222222222222222222   222   2222222222222222222222222222222222
2222222222222222222222222222222222222222   222   2222222222222222222222222222222222
2222222222222222222222222222222222222222222222222222222222222222222222222222222222
2222222222222222222222222222222222222222222222222222222222222222222222222222222222
```

The Lease Decision with Taxes

THE analysis of the previous chapter was based on a zero tax rate. We shall now assume that there is a .46 corporate income tax. All business decisions must be made on an after-tax basis and the buy versus lease decision is no exception.

Several analytical problems arise from the fact that a lease is a combination of an investment and a financing. For example, when an asset is purchased, the firm will deduct depreciation expense in computing taxable income. With a lease there is no depreciation expense, but the entire lease payment is a tax deduction. We want to separate the lease payment into two components, one an equivalent to interest on debt and the second an equivalent to depreciation expense.

If we start with the before-tax lease payment (say, $36,190 per year) equal in each year of the asset's life to the debt payment accompanying the purchase of the asset, we have indifference on a before-tax basis if there is zero residual value.

With indifference with zero taxes the preference between buying and leasing rests with the value of the tax deductions associated with interest and depreciation if the asset is purchased and the total lease payment if the asset is leased. Later we will make the choice using the depreciation deduction of buying and the depreciation equivalent of lease payments.

14

A Basic Example

Assume that the lessor offers to lease an asset at a cost of $36,190 per year, first payment one year from now. This is exactly the same cash outlay (amount and timing) as with the buy-borrow alternative. The life is three years and there is zero residual value. With a zero tax rate, there would be indifference.

With a .46 tax rate, which alternative is to be preferred? Conventional wisdom says that leasing offers tax advantages. Rather than accepting this generalization, we will compare the tax deductions of buying with leasing. The cost of the asset purchased outright is $90,000 and the leasing alternative has a before-tax present value of $90,000, using a .10 discount rate. If $90,000 were to be borrowed at a cost of 10 percent, the debt amortization schedule with equal repayments would be

Time	Amount Owed Beginning of Period	Interest at 10 Percent	Principal Payment	Total Payment
1	90,000	9,000	27,190	36,190
2	62,810	6,280	29,910	36,190
3	32,900	3,290	32,900	36,190

If the asset is purchased using borrowed funds, the total tax deductions resulting from borrowing at 10 percent and the use of straight-line depreciation are shown now with the tax deductions from leasing.

Time	Interest	Straight-Line Depreciation	Buy-Borrow Tax Deductions	Lease Tax Deductions
1	9,000	30,000	39,000	36,190
2	6,280	30,000	36,280	36,190
3	3,290	30,000	33,290	36,190
		Total tax deductions	108,570	108,570

The total tax deductions from buying and leasing are equal in this example. The timing pattern of the deductions with buying is to be preferred since the deductions are accelerated as compared with leasing. The use of any of the accelerated depreciation methods would further enhance the tax advantages of buying.

We started with zero taxes and indifference between buying and leasing. The addition of taxes moved the choice to the buy alternative. The present value of the tax deductions with buy and borrow is larger than with leasing with any positive discount rate.

tax rate = 0.046

Using the Borrowing Rate

If the borrowing rate (after taxes) is used to discount the cash flows, we can compute the after-tax costs of the two alternatives.

We define the net cost of buying to be equal to the cost minus the present value of any tax savings associated with the asset. For the example, the net cost of buying is equal to $90,000 minus the present value of the tax savings from depreciating the asset. Since the depreciation deductions of each year are equal, we will use the present value of an annuity with an interest rate of .054 (that is, .10 times one minus the tax rate) to compute the present value of the tax savings. The present value of an annuity for three years using .054 as the discount rate is 2.70296.

Net cost of buying = $90,000 - .46(30,000)(2.70296) = 90,000 - 37,301 = 52,699$

The after-tax present value of leasing is

$$36,190 (1 - .46)2.70296 = 52,823$$

Leasing costs more than buying.

The interest tax shield is omitted from the buy analysis since the inclusion of the debt flows would result in their washing out completely (the net present value of the debt flows is equal to zero) when the after-tax borrowing rate is being used as the discount rate. Their inclusion if a different rate were used would result in distortion of the investment analysis.

If an interest rate other than the after-tax borrowing rate of .054 were to be used, and if debt flows were excluded from the buy analysis, the computation of the present value of the leasing costs would be more complex than that illustrated. One can only compute the after-tax cost of leasing by computing a present value of after-tax lease payments using an annuity if the after-tax borrowing rate is used.

Timing of Lease Payments

We want to illustrate the advantage to a lessee of accelerating lease payments. A general proof is given in Appendix III to this chapter.

Imagine a situation in which the choice is between a lease payment of $100 at time 1 or a payment of $90.91 at time 0 (the borrowing rate is .10). On a before-tax basis the lessee is indifferent. On an after-tax basis using the after-tax borrowing rate of .054 with a time 1 payment of $100, we have

$$100(1 - .46) = 54$$

16

The present value of the after-tax cost = $54/1.054 = $51.23. With a time 0 payment of $90.91, we have

$$90.91 (1 - .46) = 49.09 \text{ after-tax cost}$$

The time 0 payment of $90.91 has a lower after-tax present value than does the time 1 payment of $100.

If the lessor has a .46 tax rate, the lessor will prefer the time 1 payment of $100 if all facts remain unchanged. The cash flows will be exactly as computed except that they will be revenues rather than costs.

Both the tax rates of the two parties and their discount rates (both real and perceived) will affect the preferences for the cash flow patterns. All things equal, the lessee will prefer acceleration of lease payments and the lessor will prefer deferral.

Example:

What is the after-tax cost to the lessee if there is one lease payment at time 0 of $90,000?

$$90,000(1 - .4) = 54,000$$

The IRS is apt to consider this a purchase rather than a lease, but the basic logic of the lessee paying taxes wanting accelerated leases still applies. Remember, we are assuming indifference for the lessee on a before-tax basis and a preference for acceleration by the lessee on an after-tax basis.

Accelerating the Lease Payments: The Basic Example

Instead of three lease payments of $36,190, assume that there are three beginning-of-the-period lease payments of $32,900, where $32,900 is the before-tax present value of $36,190 (that is, $36,190/1.10 = $32,900). How does this acceleration of payment affect the after-tax cost of leasing?

$$
\begin{array}{rcl}
32,900 \times 1.054^{-0} & = & 32,900 \\
32,900 \times 1.054^{-1} & = & 31,214 \\
32,900 \times 1.054^{-2} & = & \underline{29,615} \\
& & 93,729 \\
& & \underline{\times \quad .54} \\
\text{Present value of leasing} & = & 50,614
\end{array}
$$

Now, the leasing cost (50,615) is less than the buying cost ($52,699).

An acceleration of the lease payments affects the desirability of leasing as compared with buying. If lease cash flows are replaced by their before-tax present value equivalents, the lease alternative is enhanced from the viewpoint of the lessee. The before-tax present values are not changed, but the after-tax present values are. Acceleration of lease payments of this nature will reduce the after-tax present value of leasing.

Risk-Adjusted Discount Rates

If the after-tax borrowing rate is used in computing present values, the calculations of the net costs of buying and leasing are straightforward (they were illustrated earlier). If discount rates are used that attempt to reflect the existence of risk, the calculations are much more difficult. The problem is to treat leasing (which includes debt flows) and the buy analysis (which conventionally excludes debt flows) on a comparable basis. This problem is bypassed if the after-tax borrowing rate is used, but it becomes alive with any other discount rate.

Consider a one-period lease with an outlay of $1,200 at time 1. There is a .46 tax rate and funds can be borrowed at a cost of .10 (.054 after taxes) and the asset can be purchased at a cost of $1,000. Assume that the firm uses a .20 after-tax time discount factor to evaluate investments.

The after-tax lease cost is $(1 - .46)\$1,200$ or $648 at time 1. Using a discount rate of .20 the present value of the leasing cost is $648/1.20 = $540. The net cost of buying if the tax deduction for depreciation is used at time 1 is

$$\text{Net cost of buying} = 1,000 - .46(1,000)(1.20)^{-1} = 617$$

Since $540 is less than $617, it would appear that leasing costs less than does buying. However there is an error hidden in the analysis. Consider the cash flows of buying with $1,000 of borrowed funds. At time 0 there are no net cash flows (the cost of the asset equals the debt funds received). At time 1 we have for the buy-borrow alternative

Cash outlay of debt	−1,100
Tax saving of interest	46
Tax saving of depreciation	460
Cash flow of buy and borrow	−594

For the lease alternative we have at time 1

Cash outlay of lease	−1,200
Tax saving	552
Cash flow of lease	−648

At time 1 the lease alternative has a net cash outlay of $648 compared with a cash outlay of only $594 with buying. Buying is superior by $54 (at time 1). The solution was obtained by including the debt flows in the buy analysis.

The advantage of buying is seen also if the after-tax borrowing rate is used. Using .054, the $648 net after-tax cash outlay of leasing at time 1 has a present value of $648/1.054 = $615. Buying has a net cost of $1,000 − $460/1.054 = $1,000 − $436 = $564.

We can also compute the before-tax present value debt equivalent of leasing using the before-tax borrowing rate of .10, which is $1,200/1.10 = $1,091, and then deduct the present value of the tax savings that are nondebt related. The .10 interest on $1,091 is $109. The amount of deduction that is nondebt related, $1,200 − $109 = $1,091, results in a tax saving of $502 and the present value of the tax saving is $502/1.054 = $476.

We again obtain a net present value of leasing of $1,091 − $476 = $615. And the net cost of buying using .054 is again

$$1,000 - \frac{460}{1.054} = 564$$

There is a $51 present value advantage to buying.

If any of the cash flows are to be discounted at .20, the firm's required return or any other risk-adjusted discount rate, there are problems of analysis. Discounting some debt flows (lease flows) at .20 but not others (debt flows if the purchase of the asset if financed with straight debt) creates distortions in the analysis and leads to calculations that are difficult to explain. However, there is another alternative method of analysis that can be defended. We can take the previously computed $1,091 before-tax debt equivalent of the lease and deduct the present value of the tax savings (nondebt related) using the risk-adjusted rate. The tax savings were computed to be $502 at time 1. The present value of the tax savings using .20 as the discount rate is

$$\frac{502}{1.20} = 418$$

We obtain a net after-tax present value of leasing, using .20 to discount the nondebt-related tax savings of $502: $1,091 − $418 = $673. The net cost of buying using 20 percent is $1,000 − $460/1.20 = $617. The present value advantage of buying as compared with leasing is now $56:

$$673 - 617 = 56$$

The analyst might desire to use a different rate of interest than .054 or

.20 in computing the present value of the tax savings. The $1,091, present value of before-tax lease payments, would not be affected. The debt equivalent equal to the present value of the lease payment is obtained using the before-tax borrowing rates rather than a risk-adjusted rate.

Thus if some rate of interest other than the after-tax borrowing rate is used to accomplish the time discounting, complexities are introduced. We cannot then take the after-tax cash outlays of the lease and compute a present value that is comparable to other investment cash flow present values (the lease includes debt flows). With more than one time period, the error introduced by discounting the after-tax lease payments by the firm's risk adjusted required return and comparing the present value obtained with the present value of buying is well hidden.

With a cancellable lease it is not necessary to compute a debt equivalent of a lease if the firm can cancel the lease with the equivalent of a phone call. Thus the calculations are much simpler than with a noncancellable lease since the present value may be computed with no special adjustments. With a noncancellable lease we have a problem if we compute the after-tax present value of the lease using something other than the after-tax borrowing rate. The present value of leasing obtained using the unadjusted lease cash flows and a risk-adjusted discount rate is not comparable to the present value of the buy alternative's cash flows.

A Continuation of the Basic Example

When the debt flows with buy are $36,190 and they are equal to the lease payments, it is useful to isolate the depreciation deductions of the buy analysis and the deductions of leasing that are the equivalent of the depreciation deductions of the buy alternative.

Previously we computed a debt amortization schedule that split the annual payment of $36,190 into principal and interest. The tax deductions of leasing, not associated with the interest equivalent, are in the column titled "principal." These deductions are the lease equivalent to depreciation expense.

LEASE TAX DEDUCTIONS

Time	Lease Outlay	Interest	Principal	Tax Rate	Tax Savings Cash Flow of Principal Component
1	36,190	9,000	27,190	.46	12,507
2	36,190	6,280	29,910	.46	13,759
3	36,190	3,290	32,900	.46	15,134
	Total principal payments		90,000		

With the buy alternative, the tax deduction each year is $30,000 and the tax saving each year is $13,800 if straight line depreciation is used. The present value of these tax savings should be deducted from the initial cost of $90,000 to obtain a net cost of buying.

To make a comparable calculation for leasing, the present value of the tax savings from the noninterest portion of the lease payments should be deducted from the present value of the before-tax lease flows computed using the before-tax borrowing rate associated with straight debt to obtain a net cost of leasing.

The risk-adjusted discount rate is being applied here only to the tax savings of noninterest tax shields. It would also be applied to any residual value (in this example the residual value is assumed to be zero) with buying.

For the present example, Figure 2.1 shows the net costs of leasing and buying for different discount rates. The net cost of buying using .10 as the rate of discount and with straight-line depreciation expense of $30,000 per year is

$$90,000 - .46(30,000)(2.4869) = 90,000 - 34,319 = 55,681$$

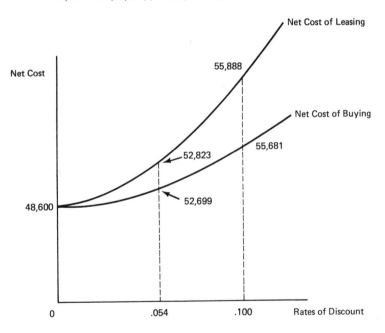

Figure 2.1

The net cost of leasing using 10 percent is

$$90,000 - .46 \left(\frac{27,190}{1.10} + \frac{29,910}{1.10^2} + \frac{32,900}{1.10^3} \right) = 90,000 - 34,112 = 55,888$$

The net cost of buying would be reduced by the present value of any residual value.

If the lease payments differed from $36,190, the before-tax present value of the lease payments would differ from $90,000 and the nondebt-related tax deductions would also differ from the numbers that have been used. It is necessary to split the lease payments into "interest" and "principal" to compute the annual tax savings if a discount rate other than the after-tax borrowing rate is used. If the after-tax borrowing rate is used, it is not necessary to make the split.

The Calculation That Is Not Made

One calculation is not made. We do not take the lease payment, multiply by one minus the tax rate to convert it to an after-tax cash flow measure, and then compute its present value using different discount rates. This calculation is correct if the after-tax borrowing rate is used, but it is not acceptable if any other discount rate is used unless the buy analysis is also adjusted to include debt flows. Including debt flows in the buy analysis is not a recommended procedure.

If the analyst were to insist on this calculation for the lease alternative, it would be necessary to include all the debt flows in the buy analysis to place it on a comparable basis.

Consider the following debt associated with buying:

Time	Interest	After-Tax Interest	Principal	After-Tax Debt Cash Flows
0				90,000
1	9,000	4,860	27,190	-32,050
2	6,280	3,391	29,910	-33,301
3	3,290	1,777	32,900	-34,677

If .054 is used as the discount rate, the present value of the debt cash flows is zero. With any discount rate larger than .054, the present value of the debt cash flow is positive. Omitting these debt cash flows from the buy analysis while including all the flows of leasing (including the tax shield from the total outlay) and using a risk-adjusted discount rate creates a bias for leasing. Both the buy and the lease analysis must be placed on a comparable basis, preferably excluding debt flows or debt tax effects from both.

The Investment Decision

We will illustrate the investment decision with and without the inclusion of debt. Assume that the investment costs $90,000 and has a life of three years. Straight-line depreciation is used. The borrowing rate is .10. The net cost of buying using .054 is

Net cost of buying = 90,000 – .46(30,000)(2.70296) = 52,699

If the cash flows of the debt are included, the net cost is not changed. The net present value of the debt cash flows is

Time	After-Tax Debt Flows	Present Value Factors (.054)	Present Values
0	90,000	1.0000	90,000
1	–32,050	$(1.054)^{-1}$	–30,408
2	–33,301	$(1.054)^{-2}$	–29,976
3	–34,677	$(1.054)^{-3}$	–29,616
			0

If the .10 is used as the discount rate, the net cost of buying without including debt is

Net cost of buying = 90,000 – .46(30,000)(2.4869) = 55,681

But using .10, the present value of the debt is a positive amount of $7,290. Thus the net cost of buying would be reduced to $48,391. A different timing of debt repayment would change the present value.

Period	Debt Flows	Present Value Factors (.10)	Present Values
0	90,000	1.0000	90,000
1	–32,050	$(1.10)^{-1}$	–29,136
2	–32,301	$(1.10)^{-2}$	–27,521
3	–34,677	$(1.10)^{-3}$	–26,053
			7,290

If .20 is used as a discount rate, the net present value of the debt is made even larger.

If the .20 is used to compute the present value of the after-tax leasing flows and debt costing 10 percent is left out of the investment (buy) cash flows, then the two alternatives are not comparable. Either the lease payments must be treated as if they were debt payments or the debt flows must be included explicitly in the buy analysis.

Cash Flows and the Rate of Discount

Analysis of buy versus lease alternatives requires that we decide on the definition of the cash flows and the rate of discount to be used. Both the cash flows and the discount rate should be on an after-tax basis. Unfortunately, this statement does not remove all ambiguity. We will first consider the definition of cash flows with a debt and then with an investment and finally with a lease.

Cash Flows and Discount Rate: Debt

Assume that $1,000 is borrowed for one year at a cost of .10. The tax rate is .46. The after-tax borrowing rate is .10(1 − .46) = .054. If the before-tax cash flows and the before-tax interest rate are used, the net present value of the cash flows is equal to zero.

$$1,000 - \frac{1,100}{1.10} = 0$$

If the after-tax cash flows and the after-tax borrowing rate of .054 is used, we again have a net present value of zero.

$$1,000 - \frac{1,100 - 46}{1.054} = 0$$

The $46 is the tax savings resulting from the $100 of interest deductions at time 1.

If the $1,054 of net cash outlays of period 1 had been discounted at the before-tax rate of .10, the net present value would have been positive and this would have been in error. Funds can be borrowed at an after-tax cost of .054, and this should be used as the discount rate for the after-tax cash flows.

If the tax deduction cannot be used, the cash outlay at time 1 becomes $1,100 and .10 becomes the appropriate rate of discount since it represents the effective cost of debt.

Cash Flows and Discount Rate: Investment

We will now assume that the firm can invest $1,000 and earn $1,150 before taxes at time 1. This is a .15 internal rate of return on a before-tax basis. Again, funds can be borrowed at a cost of .10 and the tax rate is .46. Assume that it is agreed that the analysis should be done on an after-tax basis (this simple example can be solved correctly on a before-tax basis).

The tax on $150 of income is $69, and the after-tax cash flows at time 1 are $1,081. Using the after-tax borrowing rate, the after-tax net present value is

$$-1,000 + \frac{1,081}{1.054} = 25.62$$

If we used a before-tax .10 discount rate applied to the after-tax cash flows, we would have

$$-1,000 \ + \ \frac{1,081}{1.10} = -17.27$$

The negative net present value is clearly wrong since with no uncertainty the investment is acceptable.

	Time 0	Time 1
Investment	-1,000	1,150*
Loan	1,000	-1,100*
Net before taxes		50
Less: Taxes		23
Net after taxes		27

*Before taxes.

Now assume that the actual tax is $23 (see the table). Thus the cash flows can be defined as $1,150 - $23 = $1,127 at time one.

If we apply the before-tax rate to $1,127, we obtain:

$$-1,000 \ + \ \frac{1,127}{1.10} \ = \ 24.55$$

The net present value is somewhat different from the $25.62 obtained using the after-tax cash flow for the investment without including the interest tax shield. However, the net present value is positive as was the net present value of the first calculation. While both calculations lead to the same accept or reject decision, we recommend the calculation that uses the after-tax borrowing rate and the after-tax cash flows without considering the interest tax shield. However, it should be noted that a calculation using the actual tax and the before-tax borrowing rate also gives sensible results (the same decision but a different present value).

Cash Flows and Discount Rate: Leases

The analysis for debt and an investment carries forward for leases. We recommend the use of the after-tax cash flows and the after-tax borrowing rate as a primary calculation. This does not mean that other alternatives are not feasible but, rather, that this calculation gives sensible results and is easy to define.

If it is decided that the present value of a lease should be computed using a larger discount rate than the after-tax borrowing rate, then problems arise. The use of a higher rate of discount than the after-tax borrowing rate prevents the use of the after-tax lease cash flows (the debt elements of the lease will affect the present value). The solution suggested is a two-tier calculation. First, the debt equivalent of the lease is computed on a before-tax basis using the before-tax lease payments and the borrowing rate. Second, the present value lease equivalent of the depreciation deductions computed using the risk-adjusted discount rate is subtracted from the debt equivalent of the lease. While this calculation is complex and difficult to understand, some type of adjustment of this nature is necessary.

Conclusions

The presence of taxes combined with the desire to use risk-adjusted discount rates introduces complexities into the present value calculations. It is very easy to introduce biases into the analysis without knowing that biases have been introduced.

A simple solution is to use the after-tax borrowing rate as the discount rate in buy-versus-lease analysis. Using this rate one can compute the present value of leasing by merely reducing the lease payment to an after-tax measure and applying annuity present value factor. This simplicity disappears when a rate of discount different from the after-tax borrowing rate is used.

The acceleration of lease payments was shown to enhance the leasing alternative. However, we still conclude that if buy-borrow is being compared with leasing it is necessary actually to make the present value calculations to determine which alternative is the more desirable. Safe generalizations are very rare in the area of buy-lease analysis.

Appendix I

We will use the same symbols as in Chapter 1 and in addition let

t_c = corporate tax rate

PVD = present value of depreciation deductions per dollar of investment

r = the *after-tax borrowing rate*, where $r = (1 - t_c)k_i$

R_n = the after-tax residual value at time n

With zero salvage value and no investment tax credit the net cost of buying is

$$V_B = C - (PVD)t_c C$$

With residual value of R_n and an investment tax credit of ITC, the net cost of buying is

$$V_B = C - (PVD)t_c C - ITC - R_n (1 + r)^{-n}$$

The net cost of leasing is

$$V_L = L(1 - t_c) B(n, r)$$

27

If a discount rate of j is used rather than the after-tax borrowing rate, then we have

$$V_B = C - (PVD)t_c C - ITC - R_n(1+j)^{-n}$$

and for leasing

$$V_L = L[B(n, k_i)] - t_c \sum_{i=1}^{n} P_i(1+j)^{-i}$$

where P_i is the noninterest component of the lease payments. It should be noted that the ITC can be assigned to either the lessee or lessor.

There are two interesting conclusions:

1. You cannot use $(1 - t)L[B(n, j)]$ for the present value of leasing unless $j = (1 - t)k_i = r$.
2. Several present values are linked if k_i and r are used rather than j:

$$L[B(n, k_i)] = (1 - t)L[B(n, r)] + PV \text{ of principal tax savings using } r$$

Appendix II

Leases and Taxes

We want to consider the effect of taxes on the buy versus lease decision. Let

$$C_i = \text{debt payment of the } i\text{th year}$$
$$I_i = \text{interest payment}$$
$$P_i = \text{principal payment}$$
$$d_i = \text{depreciation expense}$$

The present values of the relevant tax deductions are

$$\text{Buy-borrow:} \quad t_c \, \Sigma \, d_i(1 + r)^{-i}$$
$$\text{Leases:} \quad t_c \, \Sigma \, P_i(1 + r)^{-i}$$

We will assume that the entire cost is financed by debt and that the before-tax present value of the lease is equal to the cost of the asset (using the before-tax borrowing rate). Then

$$\Sigma \, d_i = \Sigma \, P_i = \text{cost of assets}$$

29

It can be shown that as P_i increases, d_i decreases through time. Therefore a firm prefers buy-borrow to leasing if

1. lease payments are constant,
2. lease payments begin at time 1, and
3. indifference exists with zero taxes.

Accelerate Payment: Lessee

Assume a series of lease payments. We now remove C and insert its present value equivalent, $C(1 + k_i)^{-n}$, n periods sooner. Define

$$r = (1 - t_c)k_i$$

where k_i is the before-tax borrowing rate. This situation is shown.

The relevant after-tax costs are

$$\text{Cost before shift} = (1 - t_c) C(1 + r)^{-t}$$
$$\text{Cost after shift} = (1 - t_c) [C(1 + k_i)^{-n}] (1 + r)^{-(t-n)}$$

Is $(1 + k_i)^{-n}(1 + r)^{-(t-n)} < (1 + r)^{-t}$ or $(1 + r)^n < (1 + k_i)^n$?

The question is whether the present value of the costs are reduced by the change. Since r is less than k_i, we can conclude that the present value of the cost is reduced where \$1 is replaced by $(1 + k_i)^{-n}$ n periods sooner.

Exercises

1. a. The A Company has decided to acquire a piece of equipment but has not yet decided whether to buy or to lease. The lease payments would be $126,187 paid annually at the end of each year. If purchased at a cost of $400,000, the equipment would be financed with debt costing .10, which can be repaid at any time within the four-year period. The life of the equipment is four years. The lease is a firm commitment to make four payments.

   There is no salvage value. Should the firm lease or buy-borrow? There are no taxes.

   b. Now assume a .4 tax rate and straight-line depreciation. Should the firm buy or lease?

2. a. Assume zero taxes. Equipment can be leased at $10,000 per year (first payment one year hence) for ten years or purchased at a cost of $64,177. A bank has indicated that it would be willing to make a loan of $64,177 at a cost of 10 percent. Should the company buy or lease?

   There are no uncertainties. The equipment will be used for ten years. There is zero salvage value.

   b. Now assume a marginal tax rate of .4. Assume that the funds can be obtained for 10 percent at a bank. The company uses sum-of-the-years'-digits depreciation for taxes and the after-tax borrowing rate in computing present values. Should the firm buy or lease?

3. (Continue Exercise 2)
   Now assume a marginal tax rate of .4 and that a loan can be obtained from the bank at a cost of 9 percent. Should the firm buy or lease?

4. (Continue Exercise 3)
   Assume that the lease payments of $10,000 start immediately and that they are paid at the beginning of each of the next nine years. There are ten payments. The borrowing rate is .09. Compute the present value of leasing. Compare the present value with that obtained for Exercise 3.

5. (Continue Exercise 4)
   Assume a .4 marginal tax rate.
   a. What is the present value of the debt (the liability) if the funds are borrowed at a cost of 9 percent? Assume that the payments to the bank are $10,000 per year.
   b. What is the present value of the lease payments of $10,000 (the liability).

6. (Continue Exercise 3)
   a. Include the borrowing cash flows in the buy analysis. Assume equal payments of debt. How does this change the net cost if the after-tax borrowing rate is used?
   b. Assume that the net cost of buying was computed using the cost of capital of 15 percent. Now include the borrowing cash flows. How will this change the net cost of buying (you do not have to compute the present value)?

7. You can lease a piece of equipment for $10,000 a year, first payment due immediately. The lease would run for three years (three payments and three years of use). Alternatively, you can purchase the equipment that has a life of three years for $27,355 and borrow the funds to repay

the financing from the bank at a cost of .10. The loan would be repaid by three equal payments of $11,000, the first payment being due one period from now. (The company can borrow more funds from the bank at a cost of .10 if it so desires.)

a. With a zero tax rate, should the firm buy or lease?

b. With a .4 tax rate, should the firm buy or lease? Assume that straight-line depreciation is used for taxes and that the firm uses the after-tax borrowing rate in computing present values.

8. The benefits of a plant the ABC Company is considering building are expected to be $800,000 per year before taxes. The costs of the land and plant are

Land	5,000,000
Building	10,000,000

The estimated life of the building is 30 years. The estimated value (after tax) of the land at the end of 30 years is $20,000,000. The present value of the depreciation per dollar of depreciable base is

	Rate of Discount	
	.03	.05
Sum of the years' digits	.745488	.629142
Double declining balance	.713874	.592029

The corporate tax rate is .4. The firm can borrow at .05. The firm can lease the land and building for 30 years at a cost of $700,000 per year.

Required

a. Compute the present value of buy-borrow (exclusive of the $800,000-per-year benefits).

b. Compute the present value of leasing (exclusive of the $800,000-per-year benefits).

c. Should the firm buy or lease?

9. The XZ Company can borrow funds at .10. It has a marginal tax rate of .4. It is considering buying a plant at a cost of $1,000,000 or leasing it at a cost of $101,853 per year for 20 years. The life of the plant is 20 years with zero expected salvage. It can be depreciated using a 20-year life. The implicit before-tax cost of the lease is .08 (the present value of $101,853 a year for 20 years is $1,000,000).

$PVD = (20, .06)$,	Sum of the years' digits	=	.6768
$(20, .08)$,	Sum of the years' digits	=	.60606

a. The present value of the cost of leasing is $_____ .

b. The present value of the net cost of buying is $_____ .

10. The XYZ Company has to either buy or lease a piece of new equipment. There is an investment tax credit of .10 that is available only if the equipment is purchased. The following facts apply:

Buy: Cost: $2,000,000
Life: ten years
Tax depreciation method: straight line, ten-year life

Lease: Life: ten years (a financial type of lease)
Annual payment (end of each period): $220,000

The XYZ Company can borrow funds at 10 percent and pays a corporate tax of 40 percent.

Required: Present value of

Cost of buying = _____ .

Cost of leasing = _____ .

11. The ABD Company has a .10 borrowing rate. It can buy an asset at $24,869 or lease it at $10,000 (first payment at the end of the year). The tax rate is .46. The life of the asset and the time of the lease is three years.

a. Prepare a debt amortization table for a three-year equal payment loan of $24,869.
b. Determine the nondebt-related annual tax savings with the lease.
c. Determine the net cost of leasing if .054 is used as the discount rate.
d. Determine the net cost of leasing if .10 is used as the discount rate.
e. Determine the net cost of buying if .10 is used as the discount rate and straight-line depreciation is used for tax purposes.
f. What selling price for the asset will cause the lessee to be indifferent to buying or leasing? Use .054 as the discount rate.

Solutions

1. a. Indifference: $B(4, .10) = 3.1699$; $400,000/3.1699 = \$126,187$.
   b. Buying is more desirable. The debt repayment schedule if the funds are borrowed is

Time	Starting Balance	Interest	Principal	Total
1	400,000	40,000	86,187	126,187
2	313,813	31,381	94,806	126,187
3	219,007	21,901	104,286	126,187
4	114,721	11,472	114,715	126,187

The total tax deductions of each year, assuming buy-borrow and the use of straight-line depreciation are

Time	Interest	Depreciation	Buy-Borrow Tax Deductions	Lease Tax Deductions
1	40,000	100,000	140,000	126,187
2	31,381	100,000	131,381	126,187
3	21,901	100,000	121,901	126,187
4	11,472	100,000	111,472	126,187
		Total tax deductions	504,754	504,748

The timing of buy deductions is better than $126,187 of deductions per year as would be obtained if the firm leases.

2. a. $B(10, .10) = 6.1466$; $\$64,177/6.1446 = \$10,444$. Leasing is more desirable.
   b. The gross cost of buying is $64,177.

Present value of depreciation (.06)	=	.799974
	X	64,177
		51,340
	X	.4
		20,536
Net cost of buying	=	43,641

The annual lease payment is $10,000; $B(10, .06) = 7.3601$. Net cost of leasing is

$$(1 - .4)\ 10,000\ (7.3601) = 44,161$$

Buying is more desirable.

3.
Cost of buying	= 64,177
Present value of depreciation	X .817
	52,424
	X .4
Tax saving	20,970
Net cost of buying	= 43,207

The annual payment of leasing is $10,000. The net cost of leasing is $(1 - .4)\ \$10,000\ (7.57391) = \$45,443$. With zero taxes and a borrowing rate of .09, there was indifference. The decrease in interest cost *decreased* the net cost of buying and *increased* the cost of leasing.

4. The present value is $(1 - .4)\ \$10,000 + \$6,000\ (6.9829) = \$6,000\ (7.9829) = \$47,897$; that is the present value of the cost is now higher. $B(9, .054) = 6.9829$.

5. a. Before taxes it is $\$10,000\ (6.4177) = \$64,177$. After-tax present value is still $64,177.
   b. Before taxes it is $\$10,000\ (6.4177) = \$64,177$. The after-tax present value is

$$6,000\ B(10, .054) = 6,000\ (7.57391) = 45,443$$

However, if the present value of the implicit depreciation expense tax savings are added back, $64,177 is obtained. (See the illustrative calculations following.)

Time	Beginning of Period	Interest: .09	Implicit Depreciation	Tax Savings
1	64,177	5,776	4,224	1,690
2	59,953	5,396	4,604	1,842
3	54,177			

6. a. It does not (the present value of the debt flows using the after-tax borrowing rate is zero).
   b. Including the debt flow *reduces* the net cost since the present value of these flows is positive.
7. a. PV (lease) = $\$10,000 + \$10,000(1.7355) = \$27,355.$
   PV (buy) = $\$11,000(2.4869) = \$27,355.$ There is indifference.
   b. PV (lease) = $\$6,000(1 + 1.8334) = \$17,000.$
   PV (buy) = $\$27,355 - .4(\$27,355/3)2.673 = \$17,606.$ Lease is more desirable.
8. PV (buy) = $\$15,000,000 - \$20,000,000(.412) - \$10,000,000(.4)\,(.7454)$
   $= \$3,780,000.$
   PV (lease) $= (1 - .4)(\$700,000)(19.6) = \$8,232,000.$
   PV (benefits) $= .6(\$800,000)(19.6) = \$9,400,000.$ Buy-borrow.
   The calculations use the after-tax borrowing rate. Other calculations are also acceptable.
9. PV (lease) = $(1 - .4)\$101,853\,(11.4699) = \$700,946.$
   PV (buy) = $\$1,000,000\,(1 - .6768 \times .4) = \$729,280.$ Lease has lower cost.
10. Cost of buying = $\$2,000,000 - \$200,000 - \$200,000\,(7.3601)(.4)$
    $= \$1,211,000.$
    Cost of leasing = $(1 - t_c)\,L\,[B(n,r)] = .6\,(\$220,000)7.3601 = \$972,000.$
11. a., b.

Time	Debt	Interest	Principal	Tax Saving = Principal × .46
1	24,869	2,487	7,513	3,456
2	17,356	1,736	8,264	3,801
3	9,092	909	9,091	4,182

c. The net cost of leasing is $(1 - .46)\,\$10,000\,(2.70296) = \$14,596$ where $B(3, .054) = 2,70296.$
d. The net cost of leasing is $B(3, .10) = 2.4869; L = \$10,000\,(2.4869) = \$24,869.$ The tax savings is 9,424.

$$
\begin{array}{ll}
3,456 \times 1.10^{-1} & 3,142 \\
3,801 \times 1.10^{-2} & 3,142 \\
4,182 \times 1.10^{-3} & 3,142 \\
\hline
\text{Total} & 9,424
\end{array}
$$

Net cost = 24,869 - 9,424 = 15,445

e. Present value of depreciation = $\dfrac{24,869}{3} \times 2.4869$

$$= 20,616$$
$$\times\ \ 46$$

Tax savings $= 9,483$
Net cost of buying $= 24,869 - 9,483 = 15,386$

f.
$$
C\left[1 - .46\,\left(\frac{2.70296}{3}\right)\right] = 14,596
$$
$$.5855C = 14,596$$
$$C = 24,929$$

```
33333333333333333333333333333333333333333333333333333333333333333333333333333333333
33333333333333333333333333333333333333333333333333333333333333333333333333333333333
3333333333333333333333333333333333    333    333    33333333333333333333333333333333333
3333333333333333333333333333333333    333    333    33333333333333333333333333333333333
3333333333333333333333333333333333    333    333    33333333333333333333333333333333333
3333333333333333333333333333333333    333    333    33333333333333333333333333333333333
3333333333333333333333333333333333    333    333    33333333333333333333333333333333333
3333333333333333333333333333333333    333    333    33333333333333333333333333333333333
3333333333333333333333333333333333    333    333    33333333333333333333333333333333333
3333333333333333333333333333333333    333    333    33333333333333333333333333333333333
3333333333333333333333333333333333    333    333    33333333333333333333333333333333333
33333333333333333333333333333333333333333333333333333333333333333333333333333333333
33333333333333333333333333333333333333333333333333333333333333333333333333333333333
```

Tax Implications: Some Observations

Poorly designed tax laws will tend to distort decision making. The buy versus lease decision is very much affected by the tax laws. The primary tax factors affecting the decision are (1) the depreciation tax deduction (the method of depreciation that is allowed) and (2) the limitations, if any, on the use of a lease payment as a tax shield.

Either the lessee or the lessor can use the investment tax credit; thus theoretically the present tax code causes this factor to be neutral. In practice, the lessor might not be willing to surrender the tax credit; thus it might become relevant to a lessee's decision.

First, to illustrate the importance of taxes, we shall show how the tax law distorts investment decisions. The initial example will show that an investment that just breaks even economically can become desirable on an after-tax basis.

Assume a marginal investment that can be leased for $36,190 for three years and that will earn $36,190 per year of before-tax net benefits. There is no advantage to leasing since the costs are equal to the benefits.

Assume that the cost of an investment is $90,000 and that the entire amount can be borrowed at a cost of .10. The debt payments of $36,190 are exactly equal to the before-tax benefits, so that according to the before-tax analysis it would appear that there is also no advantage to buying. To make the decision properly we have to shift to an after-tax analysis. The life of the asset is three years with no residual value. The marginal tax rate is .46.

Using the after-tax borrowing rate of .054, the net cost of buying with a tax rate of .46 and $30,000 of straight-line depreciation is

$$90,000 - .46(30,000)\ 2.70296 = 90,000 - 37,301 = 52,699$$

The 2.70296 is equal to present value of annuity: $B(n,\ r) = B(3,\ .054) = 2.70296$. The after-tax present value of the benefits is

$$(1 - .46)\ 36,190\ (2.70296) = 52,823$$

and buying is desirable on a present value basis (the net present value is equal to $124).

We can reach the same conclusion by inspecting the cash flows of each year arising from the tax effects. Each year $36,190 of net benefits will be received and the same amount of debt payments will be made. The taxable revenues and the tax shields will be as follows:

		Tax Deductions		
Time Period	Taxable Revenues	Depreciation	Interest	Total Tax Deductions
1	36,190	30,000	9,000	39,000
2	36,190	30,000	6,280	36,280
3	36,190	30,000	3,290	33,290
	108,570			108,570

Total tax deductions are equal to the total taxable revenues, but the timing of the deductions is more accelerated. This acceleration of tax deductions compared with taxable revenues is a motivation for acquiring the marginal investment.

There is an implicit assumption in this example that the early tax deductions can be used immediately to shield income from taxation because the firm has other taxable income.

Leases with Depreciation

In at least two strange situations it is possible that the lessee will be allowed to depreciate an asset for tax purposes even though the acquisition of the asset has the legal characteristics of being a lease. The advantage of being able to depreciate the asset is that the depreciation expense will be larger than the principal portion of the lease payment (the lessee can still deduct the interest component).

Lessees have been allowed to depreciate assets acquired with the use of industrial development bonds issued by tax-exempt authorities and then leased by a corporation. The second type of situation arises when a foreign company leases the asset to a U.S. firm and both the lessor and the lessee take depreciation expense (this has been called *double dipping*).

Despite the fact that oddities such as these are likely to appear from time to time, we can expect in the normal lease that a firm will be allowed to deduct the lease payment and will not be allowed to impute depreciation expense.

The Implicit Cost of Leasing

If funds are borrowed using straight debt, the corporation has an explicit cost of borrowing. It would be nice if an analogous implicit cost of debt could be determined for a lease, with an exact economic interpretation.

Assume a zero tax situation in which the cost of the investment is $90,000 and the asset can be leased at a cost of $36,829 per year. The implicit cost of leasing is j, where

$$90,000 = 36,829B(3,j)$$

$B(3, j)$ is the present value of an annuity for three periods at j interest rate and

$$B(3,j) = 2.4437$$

Using present value tables, we find that the implicit cost of the lease, j, is .11.

The implicit interest cost of the lease in this situation is .11. In the zero tax situation the implicit cost of leasing is exactly defined and is determined relatively easily since it is exactly analogous to the cost of debt with straight debt. If the implicit cost of leasing exceeds the cost of straight debt, straight debt is more desirable. With taxes introduced, the definition of the implicit interest cost of leasing is more complex. There is not likely to be uniform agreement as to the definition. Appendix I to this chapter gives an algebraic interpretation of the implicit cost of leasing.

Assume that an asset can be purchased at a cost of $419,250. It has a ten-year life. The lease payments are $100,000 per year. The firm uses an after-tax borrowing rate of .054 to discount depreciation tax savings. What is the implicit cost of leasing? We will find the interest rate that causes the present value of the after-tax lease flows to be equal to the net cost of buying. The tax rate is .46. Using straight-line depreciation and .054 to discount the depreciation tax savings, the net cost of buying is

$$\text{Net cost of buying} = 419{,}250 - .46\left(\frac{419{,}250}{10}\right)7.57391$$

$$= 419{,}250 - 146{,}067 = 273{,}183$$

The after-tax cost of leasing per year is \$54,000. If we define j to be the after-tax implicit cost of leasing, we have

$$273{,}183 = 54{,}000B(10, j)$$
$$B(10, j) = 5.0589$$
$$j = .14+$$

The after-tax borrowing rate was used in this example to compute the present value of the depreciation tax savings. One could argue that the same discount rate should be used to discount the lease and the depreciation tax savings; therefore the implicit cost of leasing should be used to compute the present value of the depreciation tax savings.

Table 3.1 shows that the implicit rate of interest that equates the net cost of buying and the present value of leasing is .117. The significance of this number is not obvious.

TABLE 3.1   Computation of Implicit Cost of Leasing

j	$B(10, j)$	$t(PVD)C$ $.46(41{,}925)B(10, j)$	*Net Cost of Buying* $C - t(PVD)C$	$(1 - t)L[B(n, j)]$ $54{,}000B(10, j)$
.10	6.1446	118,502	300,748	331,808
.11	5.8892	113,576	305,674	318,017
.117*	5.7203	110,319	308,931	308,895
.12	5.6502	108,967	310,283	305,111
.14	5.2161	100,595	318,655	281,669

*Implicit cost of leasing (after taxes) is .117.

In Chapter 2 we argued that the after-tax cost of leasing (\$54,000) can only be discounted using the after-tax borrowing rate. If any other rate is used, the debt of leasing is being treated differently from the debt of buying. One solution is to include the debt flow with the buy alternative.

Define the term "Debt" to be the present value of debt flows associated with buying using j as the discount rate if C of cost is raised by its issuance. We then have C replaced by "Debt" for the present value of buying and we have

$$\text{Debt} - t_c(PVD)C = (1 - t_c)L[B(n, j)]$$

The problem with this formulation is that the timing of the debt payments with buying will now affect the implicit cost of leasing.

Other interpretations of the after-tax implicit cost of leasing are possible. None is very satisfactory since leasing includes a debt element, and the debt is conventionally excluded from the buy analysis. One attractive solution is to not use the concept of the implicit cost of leasing at all.

Financial Accounting Standard 13 defines the implicit cost j to be

$$\text{Fair value} - ITC = L\,[B(n, j)]$$

For the example given, the asset has a fair value of \$419,250 and there is a 10 percent investment tax credit, we have

$$419{,}250 - 41{,}925 = 100{,}000B(10, j)$$
$$B(10, j) = 3.773$$

The value of j is approximately .23.

The omission of the depreciation tax savings of the buy alternative and the use of the before-tax lease payment means that a before-tax discount rate is being computed, but deducting the investment tax credit contradicts this.

Assume a situation in which the before-tax present value of the lease stream using the borrowing rate is exactly equal to the cost of the asset. We now define the net cost of leasing in terms of its before-tax present value minus the tax savings of the nondebt element. We have

Before-tax cost of buying = before-tax present value of leasing

After taxes we have the net cost of buying equal to the net cost of leasing

$$C - t(PVD) = \text{before-tax present value of leasing} - \text{present}$$
value of tax savings of leasing from nondebt
elements only

Since the before-tax present value of leasing is equal to C, subtracting C

$$PVD = \text{present value of tax savings of leasing from}$$
non-debt elements

There is no single positive rate of interest for discounting both depreciation (straight line or accelerated) and lease tax savings that will satisfy this equation. The interest rate for the lease tax savings must be different from the interest rate used to discount the depreciation tax deductions unless the interest rate is zero. In this very reasonable situation, if we used the same rate for discounting the lease payments and the depreciation tax savings, the implicit interest cost of leasing would not be operationally useful. We could switch to a before-tax calculation, but given the importance of the tax deductions to the decision, this does not seem to be reasonable. If a given rate is used to compute the present value of depreciation, the rate used to compute the present value of tax savings of leasing will have to be smaller than the rate used for depreciation. One reaches the conclusion that, with taxes, the implicit cost of leasing is not a useful concept or calculation.

Buy versus Lease: Tax Rate Differentials

It is frequently assumed that high tax entities should own assets and that low tax entities should lease them. The basic logic is that a zero tax lessee cannot use the investment tax credit and the tax depreciation expense shields, whereas a high tax entity can protect income using these shields. For example,

> ...by separating ownership and use, leasing offers the potential of reducing the combined tax bill of lessor and lessee. In a similar manner, leasing offers companies that are unable to take full advantage of their investment tax credits a way to in effect sell them to others who can benefit from them more completely.[1]

We shall see that the generalizations regarding tax rates and leases are very complex and that the only reliable course of action is for the lessee to compute the after-tax present values of the buy and lease alternatives. There is no question that differences in tax rates for lessees and lessors are important. For example,

> We have shown the importance of different tax rates for lessees vs. lessors, particularly when interest rates are high and accelerated depreciation is allowed for tax purposes. However, saving taxes seems to be the only motive that is both obvious and substantial.[2]

Others also state the importance of the tax rates but do not explicitly cite the importance of interest rate differences:

> In short, tax factors encourage the choice between leasing and purchasing which minimizes the total taxes associated with the asset's use and ownership (ownership by the user with purchase or by the lessor with lease). Whether lease or purchase is preferred on the basis of tax considerations depends on such factors as the lessor's and lessee's tax brackets, the method of depreciating the asset (straight line, sum of the years' digits, etc.), and the degree to which the asset is debt financed by

---

[1] R. C. Higgins, *Financial Management*, Science Research Associates, Inc. (Chicago: 1977), p. 311.

[2] S. C. Myers, D. A. Dill, and A. J. Bautista, "Valuation of Financial Lease Contracts," *The Journal of Finance*, Vol. XXXI, No. 3 (June 1976), 815.

its owner (the user under purchase or the lessor under a lease). These factors vary from case to case and the impact of taxes will therefore depend on the particular situation.[3]

It will be shown that differences in discount rates is also an important factor in determining the relative merits of buying versus leasing.

We assume that a possibility exists for there to be a difference between the after-tax discount rates of the lessee and the lessor if only because of the difference in tax rates (for example, the after-tax borrowing rates will differ if the firms have the same borrowing rate and different tax rates).

The Model

We want to determine whether a zero tax firm should buy or lease (we shall call the zero tax firm the lessee). The life of the asset is n years and there is zero residual value.

Define K to be the annual cash flow (outlay) of the lessee to repay the debt if the asset is purchased and $B(n, j)$ to be the present value of an annuity for n periods and j interest rate. If C is the initial cost of the asset and j is the borrowing rate, we have for the prospective lessee

$$K[B(n, j)] = C$$

or

$$K = \frac{C}{B(n, j)}$$

In the formulation K is the annual cash outlay to repay the debt if the asset is purchased. It is the largest amount the lessee would pay each period as a lease payment since buying is an alternative.

We will now consider the position of the lessor's paying taxes at a rate of t to establish the revenues necessary for the lessor to be willing to acquire the asset and lease it to the lessee. We will assume initially that the lessor and the lessee have the same discount rate.

Assume there is no investment tax credit or residual value.

Let R be the cash the lessor must receive to break even on an after-tax basis; then

$$(1 - t)R[B(n, j)] = C[1 - (PVD)t]$$

---

[3]L. D. Schall and C. W. Haley, *Introduction to Financial Management* (New York: McGraw-Hill, 1977), p. 602.

where PVD is the present value of depreciation per dollar of cost. Solving for R;

$$R = \frac{C[1 - (PVD)t]}{(1 - t)B(n, j)}$$

The lessee will buy if K is less than R; otherwise the decision is to lease.

Let us assume that both the lessee and the lessor have zero discount rates (zero borrowing rates). An asset costs $90,000 and has a life of three years. The lessor has a .46 tax rate. The lessee with a zero tax rate would have $30,000-per-year outlays if it purchased or leased on an indifference basis.

$$K\,B(n, j) = C$$
$$3K = 90,000$$
$$K = 30,000$$

The lessor wants to break even. That is,

$$(1 - .46)R(3) = 90,000[1 - (1).46]$$
$$R = 30,000$$

Even though the lessee and lessor have different tax rates, there is no advantage to the high entity's owning the asset. The lessor would require a lease payment of $30,000, which is the same cost to the lessee that occurs if the lessee purchases the asset. The advantage of the depreciation tax shield to the lessor is exactly balanced by the taxes paid by the lessor on the lease revenues. The differential tax rates are not a sufficient factor to create an advantage for leasing.

If there were an investment tax credit that only the lessor would use, this would shift the advantage to leasing (the net cost of the asset to the lessor would be reduced).

We can generalize beyond this example. Whenever the lessee and lessor have the same discount rate, the differential in tax rates is not sufficient to create an advantage for leasing. The prospective lessee will be at least as well off buying as leasing. This is shown in Appendix II.

We find that, if the lessor has a larger tax rate than the lessee and a lower time value factor, then leasing may have an advantage to the lessee. The investment tax credit increases the likelihood that the lessee and lessor may have their positions improved by a leasing contract. Also, if the lessee and lessor agree on a mutually beneficial arrangement then leasing may be desirable independent of the discount rates. This implies lease revenues are minimized and the lessor essentially buys the tax deductions. This arrangement is consistent with the 1981 Tax Recovery Act.

An Example

We shall follow one basic example changing assumptions for successive calculations. The investment tax credit is assumed to be zero so that the calculations and formulations may be simplified.

The asset costs $1,000,000 and the sum-of-the-years'-digits depreciation is used for tax purposes. The lessor has a tax rate of .7 and the lessee has a zero tax rate. The economic and tax life of the asset is 40 years with zero residual value. If the prospective lessee buys, we assume that the purchase is financed with debt.

We will first consider the extreme case where the discount rate is zero. Both the lessor and the lessee have zero lending and borrowing rates. With buying, the debt payments are:

$$K = \frac{C}{B(n, j)}$$

$$K = \frac{1,000,000}{B(40, 0)} = \frac{1,000,000}{40} = 25,000$$

For the lessor we have

$$R = \frac{C\,[1 - (PVD)t\,]}{(1 - t)B(n, j)}$$

where

$$PVD = 1, t(PVD) = .7$$
$$B(n, j) = 40$$
$$1 - t = .3$$

$$R = \frac{1,000,000\,(1 - .7)}{.3(40)} = 25,000$$

In this example, where the time value factor is equal to zero, K equals R and the lessee is indifferent between buying the asset for $1,000,000 and paying the $25,000 a year to repay the debt associated with the asset and paying the lessor $25,000 per year. This indifference occurs even though the lessee has a zero tax rate and the lessor has a .7 tax rate.

The advantage of the depreciation tax saving to the lessor is exactly balanced by the fact that the revenues of the lessor are taxed. The differential between the lessor and the lessee's tax rates is not a sufficient factor to create a motivation for leasing, if there are no special arrangements between the lessor and lessee.

The net cost of buying to a lessor with a .7 tax rate and a zero rate of discount is

$$1,000,000 - .7(1,000,000) = 300,000$$

where .7(1,000,000) is the tax savings from the depreciation tax shield.

The lessor receives $25,000 of lease revenues but only has $7,500 after taxes. There are 40 payments, so the lessor receives 7,500 × 40 = $300,000 and just breaks even.

An investment tax credit that only went to the lessor would change the conclusion. For example, a .10 investment tax credit would result in

$$(1 - .7)R(40) = 1,000,000 (1 - .7 - .1)$$
$$12R = 200,000$$
$$R = 16,667$$

The lease payment per year must now be $16,667 for the lessor to break even. The cost of buying for the zero tax lessee is $25,000 per year; thus leasing at a cost of $16,667 is to be preferred.

The Same Discount Rate

With a zero investment tax credit in which the lessor and the lessee both have the same after-tax discount rate, the lessee is always at least as well off buying as leasing. Since the conclusion is independent of the magnitude of the tax rate of the lessor (as long as it is positive), it is a surprise. A proof follows for the situation where the after-tax borrowing rate is being used for the discount rate.

We want to determine if

$$R \geqslant K$$

or

$$\frac{C[1 - (PVD)t]}{(1 - t)B(n, j)} \geqslant \frac{C}{B(n, j)}$$

Simplifying

$$1 - (PVD)t > (1 - t)$$

Since PVD is less than one, the inequality holds and the left-hand side exceeds the right. The lessor requires a larger lease payment than the lessee would have to pay if the lessee purchases the asset. The conclusion results when both entities are using the same after-tax discount rate.

This inequality results since the discount rates for the lessee and lessor are equal. For example, if $j = .20$ we have for the lessee

$$K = \frac{C}{B(40, .20)} = \frac{1,000,000}{4.9966} = 200,000$$

For the lessor, we have

$$R = \frac{C[1 - (PVD)t]}{(1 - t)B(40, .20)} = \frac{1,000,000\,[1 - (.2134).7]}{.3 \times 4.996} = 567,000$$

The prospective lessee has an incentive to buy rather than to lease since the lessor must charge \$567,000 per year whereas the cost of the prospective lessee of buying is only \$200,000.

An inclusion of a .10 investment tax credit does not alter the relative desirability of buying for this example, although the value of R decreases:

$$R = \frac{1,000,000(1 - .7 \times .213435 - .1)}{.3(4.9966)} = 500,000$$

Different Discount Rates

Before the 1981 tax act tax rate differentials and differences in discount rates were necessary (we are, of course, not considering all the other possible motivations for leasing such as different expectations), if leasing were to be desirable to both the lessee and lessor.

Let k = the discount rate of the lessee and r = the discount rate of the lessor (after tax). Leasing is desirable if

$$\frac{C}{B(n, k)} > \frac{C\,[1 - (PVD)t]}{(1 - t)B(n, r)}$$

or equivalently if

$$B(n, r) > \frac{[1 - (PVD)t]\,B(n, k)}{(1 - t)}$$

Table 3.2 shows the annual cash flows (outlays) required by the lessee for buying and leasing from a lessor with a .7 tax rate. The asset has a 40-year life and costs \$1,000,000. The lessee has a zero tax rate.

TABLE 3.2 ANNUAL COST TO LESSEE IF LESSOR BREAKS EVEN; LESSEE HAS ZERO TAX RATE

Interest Cost to		Cost to Firm Wanting Use of Asset	
Lessee: k	Lessor: r	Buys	Leases
0	0	25,000	25,000
.10	.03	102,000	74,920
.10	.042	102,000	102,000
.10	.06	102,000	143,000
.10	.10	102,000	253,000
.20	.20	200,000	567,000

Interest Rate Relationships

The possibility of investing in tax-exempt securities, deferring taxes, and converting ordinary income to capital gains makes the determination of discount rates for different entities taxed at different rates very complex. We will simplify the analysis by assuming that the lessee has zero taxes and has a cost of money of k. The lessor has a tax rate of t and cost of money of r where

$$r = (1 - t)k$$

Continuing the example, assume that $k = .10$ and $t = .7$ for the lessor. Now r is equal to .03. The asset should be leased if the lessee also borrows at .10 and thus has a time value factor of .10. The lessor has an after-tax time value factor of .03, that is

$$r = (1 - t)k = (1 - .7).10 = .03$$

The net after-tax cost of acquiring the asset to the lessor is

$$\text{Net cost} = 1,000,000 - .7(.686391)1,000,000$$
$$= 519,526$$

The present value of the depreciation deductions, per dollar of cost, using .03, is .686391.

We will show that $74,920 is the minimum lease payment the lessor will accept.

If the lessee pays $74,920 per year, the lessor's after-tax revenues are $(1 - .7)$74,920 = $22,476 per year. Since $B(40, .03) = 23.11477$, the present value of the after-tax revenues is

$$PV \text{ (revenues)} = 22,476(23.11477) = 519,526$$

48

This is exactly equal to the net after-tax cost.

The lessor is willing to rent the asset at a minimum price of $74,920. We are assuming that the lessor does not buy the asset until the lease is signed. The lessee can buy the asset at an annual cost of $102,000 based on an interest rate for the lessee of .10.

The difference between the maximum the lessee is willing to pay to lease ($102,000) and the minimum the lessor is willing to accept ($74,920) can be bargained for by the two parties.

If for any reason (such as opportunities to invest in tax-exempt securities) the lessor's discount rate were higher than .03, the lease revenues required by the lessor would increase (see Table 3.2). If the discount rates of the lessee and lessor were both .10, the minimum revenue requirements of the lessor would be $253,000, and at that level of charge the lessee would have a strong incentive to purchase. If the lessor has a discount rate a little larger than .042, the lessor would require an amount per year equal to the annual cost to the lessee, if the lessee purchased the asset. At that cost the lessee would be indifferent to leasing or buying the asset.

We have assumed that the lessee has a zero tax rate. Changing that assumption will not change the basic conclusions, but it will change the calculations being made for the lessee. We have also assumed that the lessor will discount the tax savings from depreciation deductions at the same rate as the after-tax lease revenues are discounted. The assumption seems to be reasonable, but other assumptions are possible.

Leveraged Leasing

Leveraged leasing makes the analysis more complex by splitting the lessor's financing between equity and debt contributors. The two sources of capital are likely to have different tax rates as well as different costs. Generalizations in this setting would be very difficult.

Conclusions

Based on the analysis it is concluded that we cannot always assume that low-tax investors should lease and that high-tax investors should be lessors. The choice of the optimum actions of the several parties will depend heavily on the discount rates that are being used by the lessee and lessor, as well as their tax rates, and what type of arrangements the tax laws will allow.

The analysis has assumed that the prospective lessee has zero taxes. A change in this assumption would not change the basic conclusion that the net cost of the two alternatives must be computed and that both the tax rate differences between lessee and lessor as well as the discount rates play an important part in determining the relative desirability of the buy and lease alternatives.

We have also assumed that the lessee is indifferent to making payments to a bank if the asset is purchased and financed with debt or to a lessor if the asset is leased. This assumes that failure to pay triggers the same consequences in both situations. The risk and costs of bankruptcy are assumed not to change.

A differential in tax rates creates the possibility that the lessee and lessor may both benefit from a leasing arrangement. To determine whether or not leasing is more beneficial than buying, it is necessary for the lessee to make the correct present value calculations. Even where the situation (tax rates and discount rates) is such that one could expect leasing arrangement to be mutually beneficial, this cannot be assumed. Greed or incorrect assumption and calculations on the part of the lessor might still dictate buying by the prospective lessee. The same factors might also lead to a decision to buy even though there are institutional factors (such as interest rates and tax rates) that would lead one to assume that leasing would be more desirable.

The 1981 Tax Recovery Act has given rise to the possibility of one party (the low tax entity) selling the tax deductions to a high tax entity. While the arrangement might still be called a lease, it is not consistent with the definition of lease used in this chapter.

Appendix I

The Implicit Cost of a Lease

The Before-Tax Cost

Let C be the cost of the asset if purchased, L be the annual lease payment, and k be the implicit cost of leasing. Then if the asset has a life of n years, $C = L[B(n, k)]$ and $B(n, k) = C/L$. We can then solve for j.

The After-Tax Cost

One way of defining the implicit after-tax cost of leasing, j, is

$$C - t(PVD)C = (1 - t)L[B(n, j)]$$

or

$$\frac{C}{L} = \frac{(1 - t)B(n, j)}{1 - t(PVD)}$$

where PVD is equal to the present value of depreciation expense per dollar of depreciable base. We can use this relationship to solve for j, but the use of $L(1 - t)B(n, j)$ when j is not equal to the after-tax borrowing rate is not justifiable.

Appendix II

With the same discount rate being used by both the lessee and lessor, we want to determine if

$$\frac{C[1 - (PVD)t]}{(1 - t)B(n, j)} \geq \frac{C}{B(n, j)}$$

or

$$1 - (PVD)t \geq 1 - t$$

Since *PVD* is less than 1, the inequality holds and the left-hand side exceeds the right. The lessor requires a larger lease payment than the lessee would have to pay if the asset were purchased.

Exercises

1. An investment will give $10,000 a year benefits for three years (no residual value). It can be leased for $10,000 a year. The tax rate is .46. Funds can be borrowed at a cost of .10. The firm uses its borrowing rate to discount for time.
   a. Should it be leased?
   b. Should it be purchased at a cost of $24,869? Use straight-line depreciation.

c. Prepare a debt amortization table and show the tax deductions of
each year with purchase.

2. A lease is three years long. The firm can borrow at .10. The lessee can
pay $10,000 at the end of each year or $9,091 at the beginning of each
of three years. The firm uses its borrowing rate to discount for time.
   a. With zero taxes, which lease arrangement will the lessee prefer?
   b. With a tax rate of .46, which lease arrangement will the lessee prefer?

3. (Continue Exercise 2)
   a. With a zero tax rate, which lease arrangement will the lessor prefer?
   The lessor borrows at a cost of .10.
   b. With a .46 tax rate, which lease arrangement will the lessor prefer?
   c. Under what circumstances will the lessee and lessor readily agree that
   $9,091 at the beginning of each period is to be preferred?

4. There are zero taxes. What is the implicit cost of leasing if the asset can
be purchased at a cost of $419,250 and the lease payments are $100,000
per year for ten years?

5. Determine the implicit cost of leasing for Exercise 1. Use straight-line depreciation and the after-tax borrowing rate to discount the depreciation
tax savings. The implicit cost of leasing should only be used to discount
the after-tax cost leasing.

6. The prospective lessee can buy an asset for $24,869. The lessee has a zero
tax rate and can borrow funds at a cost of .10. The asset has a life of
three years. The lessor has a .46 tax rate. It can also acquire the asset at a
cost of $24,869. It uses straight-line depreciation.
   a. What is the annual cost to the lessee of buying the asset?
   b. What lease rental does the lessor have to charge to break even? It can
   borrow at .10 and uses a .054 discount rate.
   c. What lease rental does the lessor have to charge to break even if it uses
   a discount rate of .10?

Solutions

1. a. No. The benefits are exactly equal to the lease costs.
   b. $B(3, .054) = 2.70296$.

$$\text{Net cost} \quad = 24,869 - .46(\frac{24,869}{3})2.70296$$

$$= 24,869 - 10,307 = 14,562$$

$$PV \text{ (benefits)} = (1 - .46)10,000(2.70296) = 14,596$$

Buying is marginally desirable.

c.

Time	Debt	Interest	Principal Payment	Debt: End of Period
1	24,869	2,487	7,513	17,356
2	17,356	1,736	8,264	9,092
3	9,092	909	9,091	0

Time	Tax Deductions: Buy		Taxable Income		
	Interest	Depreciation	Total		Difference
1	2,487	8,290	10,777	10,000	777
2	1,736	8,290	10,026	10,000	26
3	909	8,290	9,199	10,000	-801

2. a. Indifferent.

$$10,000 \, B(3, .10) = 10,000(2.4869) = 24,869$$
$$9,091[1 + B(2, .10)] = 9,091(2.7355) = 24,869$$

   b. $9,091 for three years.

$$10,000 \, (1 - .46)(2.70296) = 14,596$$
$$9,091 \, (1 - .46)(2.84892) = 13,986$$

   where $B(2, .054) = 1.84892$

3. a. Indifferent.
   b. The $10,000 per year at the end of each year.
   c. Lessee pays taxes and the lessor does not.

4.

$$100,000B(10, j) = 419,250$$
$$B(10, j) = 4.19250$$
$$j = .20$$

5. $C - t_c \, (PVD)C = (1 - t_c)L \, [B(n, j_t)]$.

$$24,869 - .46 \left(\frac{2.70296}{3}\right) 24,869 = (1 - .46)10,000B(3, j_t)$$

$$14,562 = 5,400B(3, j_t)$$
$$B(3, j_t) = 2.69667$$
$$j_t = .055+$$

Other interpretations of the implicit cost of leasing are possible.

6. a. $B(3, .10) = 2.4869$; $24,869/2.4869 = $10,000$.
   b.

$$24,869 - .46 \left(\frac{2.70296}{3}\right) 24,869 = 14,562$$

$$(1 - .46)B(3, .054)R = 14,562$$

$$R = \frac{14,562}{.54(2.70296)} = 9,977$$

   c.

$$(1 - .46) \left(\frac{24,869}{3}\right)B(3, .10) = (1 - .46)B(3, .10)R$$

$$R = 15,351$$

```
4444444444444444444444444444444444444444444444444444444444444444444444444444444
4444444444444444444444444444444444444444444444444444444444444444444444444444444
44444444444444444444444444444   444   444444444444   44444444444444444444444444
44444444444444444444444444444   4444   44444444444   44444444444444444444444444
44444444444444444444444444444   44444   444444444   444444444444444444444444444
44444444444444444444444444444   444444   4444444   4444444444444444444444444444
44444444444444444444444444444   4444444   44444   44444444444444444444444444444
44444444444444444444444444444   44444444   444   444444444444444444444444444444
44444444444444444444444444444   44444444   4   4444444444444444444444444444444
44444444444444444444444444444   444444444    44444444444444444444444444444444
44444444444444444444444444444   44444444444   444444444444444444444444444444
4444444444444444444444444444444444444444444444444444444444444444444444444444444
4444444444444444444444444444444444444444444444444444444444444444444444444444444
```

Accounting for Leases

Up to this point it has been implied that the buy versus lease decision should be made strictly on the basis of economic valuation. A business manager is more likely to base the decision on a complete set of considerations, including the financial accounting measures that will result from the decision.

In this chapter we will consider the effects of the buy versus lease decision on the balance sheet and the income statement of a firm. While it can be argued that a sophisticated financial analyst will reconstruct financial statements to take into consideration leases that have not been recorded, many business managers believe that the omission of leases from the balance sheet is of significant value.

The buy or lease decision leads to two types of effects. One is the omission of a lease from the financial position reports (balance sheets). This omission can readily be adjusted for if the information is available by imputing a present value of the liability. The second is the fact that the income measures will be affected by the choice to buy or lease (the income measures may also be affected by accounting conventions).

In 1980 one of the *Fortune* 500 corporations that had until then been classified as a growth company underwent a period of flat earnings. Top management panicked at the prospect of an earnings decrease and cut back drastically on capital expenditures. As a result, middle management (or, more exactly, all managers not directly in charge of the capital expenditure cutback program) then proceeded to lease assets (they were prevented by fiat from buying) as long as the leases were not capital leases. A capital lease would have been considered an asset (and a liability) equivalent to a purchase and thus would have come under the capital expenditure limitation. Interestingly, the decision to lease might have actually benefited the accounting incomes of the first year or two even if the decision to lease were not economically desirable.

FAS 13

Prior to statement 13 (FAS 13) of the Financial Accounting Standards Board, except for leases that were essentially purchases (as defined in APB 5), there was no requirement that leases be shown as liabilities. FAS 13 changed the accounting treatment of leases. We can expect to see additional changes in the future.

FAS 13 gives the lessee two basic choices as to how leases should be accounted for. A lease is either classified as a *capital* or *operating* lease. It is a capital lease if any one of the following four conditions applies:

1. The asset's ownership is transferred from the lessor to lessee.
2. The lessee has an option to purchase the asset at bargain price.
3. The lease term is equal to or greater than .75 of the life of the asset.
4. The present value of the rentals is equal to or greater than .9 of the fair value minus investment tax credit (fair value refers to normal selling price).

If the lease qualifies as a capital lease, an asset and liability are recorded and are shown on the balance sheet. If none of the above conditions is satisfied, the lease is an operating lease and the lease is not recorded as a liability or an asset.

Example:

$B(10, .10) = 6.1446$, the cost of borrowing is equal to .10

Fair value = $800,000	Lease =	$100,000/year
Life = 20 years	Lease =	10 years

There is no ownership transfer and no option to buy at a bargain price. Is the lease a capital lease?

1. There is no ownership transfer.
2. There is no option to buy at a bargain price.
3. The lease term of 10 years is not greater than .75 of the 20-year life.
4. The present value of the lease ($614,000) is not greater than .9 of the $800,000 fair value. There is zero investment tax credit.

If any one of the four criteria had been satisfied (if one of the statements had been affirmative rather than negative), the lease would have been a capital lease. None of the four basic conditions is satisfied; therefore it is an operating lease.

Accounting for Capital Leases

If the lease is classified as a capital lease, an asset and liability are recorded. The asset is then depreciated using the firm's normal depreciation method, and the liability is amortized as the debt (lease) payments are made.

Thus a capital lease will add to a firm's debt, and its inclusion will adversely affect any debt ratios that are computed. In addition, the incomes of each period will be affected by the fact that the lease is a capital lease.

We shall illustrate the accounting for capital leases using a simplified example.

An Accounting Example

Take $n = 3$, $t_c = .46$, cost of debt $= .10$, and $r = .054$ where $(1 - .46).10 = .054$. If $90,000 is borrowed, with payments of $36,190 each year, the equal payment debt amortization table will be

Time	Debt at Beginning of Period	Interest: .10	Reduction in Principal	Debt at End of Period
1	90,000	9,000	27,190	62,810
2	62,810	6,280	29,910	32,900
3	32,900	3,290	32,900	0
			90,000	

The before-tax present value of the debt payments using the before-tax borrowing rate is $90,000. The after-tax present value of the after-tax debt payments is also $90,000 using .054 as the discount rate.

	Present Value
1. $[9,000(1 - .46) + 27,190]\ 1.054^{-1}$ =	30,408
2. $[6,280(1 - .46) + 29,190]\ 1.054^{-2}$ =	29,976
3. $[3,290(1 - .46) + 32,900]\ 1.054^{-3}$ =	29,616
Present value of debt =	90,000

Assume the lease is a capital lease in which both the benefits and the lease payments are $36,190 at the end of each year. The present value of the lease payments is $90,000. FAS 13 requires that the following initial entry or its equivalent be made:

Asset: Leasehold	90,000	
Liability: Leases		90,000

FAS 13 recommends the use of the firm's normal depreciation calculation for a capital lease. The following entries are appropriate for the operations of year 1 if straight-line depreciation expense is used by the firm:

Depreciation expense	30,000	
Asset: Leasehold		30,000
Liability: Leases	27,190	
Interest expense	9,000	
Bank		36,190

The total expenses are $39,000, which is greater than the lease payments of $36,190. The application of FAS 13 causes the earnings of the early years of life to be depressed if the lease is a capital lease compared with the income that would result if the lease were an operating lease. The sum of the depreciation expense and the interest with a capital lease is likely to be larger than the lease payment in the early years of the lease.

All things equal, a corporation is likely to prefer that a lease be classified as an operating lease rather than as a capital lease. A capital lease adversely affects debt-equity ratios and in addition depresses the incomes of the early years of the lease. Over the life of the asset (or lease contract), the effects on income of the lease classification will balance out, but that is little consolation to a manager concerned with the short run so that he or she can survive long enough to participate in the long run.

An Alternative Approach

FAS 13 is an important step toward improved financial reporting in that a lease liability is now recorded for some leases. However, it is not clear that the use of normal depreciation is appropriate. We will consider an alternative approach to writing off the asset and recording the depreciation expense.

The asset consists of the after-tax present value of $36,190 cash flows (the benefits) per period plus the present value of the tax savings of the principal component of the lease payments. Debt components of the lease are not included. We have

	Present Values at Time n		
	0	*1*	*2*
$(1 - .46)36,190\,B(n, .054)$	52,823	36,133	18,541
Tax savings of the "principal" payments			
$27,190 \times .46 = 12,567.40$	11,867		
$29,910 \times .46 = 13,758.60$	12,385	13,054	
$32,900 \times .46 = 15,134.00$	12,925	13,623	14,359
Present value	90,000	62,810	32,900

We will define the depreciation to be equal to the change in value.

Depreciation of year 1 = 90,000 – 62,810 = 27,190
Depreciation of year 2 = 62,810 – 32,900 = 29,910
Depreciation of year 3 = 32,900 – 0   = 32,900

The total expenses (interest plus depreciation) are

Time	Depreciation	Interest	Total Expenses	Cash Payment of Leases
1	27,190	9,000	36,190	36,190
2	29,910	6,280	36,190	36,190
3	32,900	3,290	36,190	36,190

Using this alternative method of computing expenses, there is no longer a bias against the incomes of the early years using a capital lease procedure as there is with the normal depreciation method used for capital leases with FAS 13.

The entry to record the lease could be

Asset: Leasehold	90,000	
Liability: Lease		90,000

After one time period the following entries or their equivalent would be made:

Interest expense	9,000	
Depreciation expense	27,190	
Asset: Leasehold		27,190
Liability: Lease		9,000
Liability: Lease	36,190	
Cash		36,190

Comparable entries would be made for the other two years.

Following this procedure, a capital lease and an operating lease would have the same expenses each period. However, the expenses with leasing would be different from the expenses that would occur if the asset were to be purchased at a cost of $90,000 and normal straight-line or accelerated depreciation used.

Capital and Operating Leases: A Recommendation

Currently four conditions may be applied to determine if a lease is a capital lease or an operating lease. They are sensible, but they are unnecessary. The present value of all leases with durations in excess of one year could be shown as liabilities. The sole criterion would be whether or not there is a legal obligation of the lessee to pay in the future. In a sense the .75 of the life requirement would be lowered to a small number as would the requirement that the present value of the rentals be equal to or greater than .9 of the fair value. By sufficiently lowering the .9, we cause all leases to be capital leases.

Rather than defining a capital lease to be one in which substantially all the benefits and risks are transferred from the lessor to the lessee, the focus would be on recording the present value of those benefits that are transferred, even if they are a small percentage of the total value of the asset.

FAS 13 is complex and difficult to implement. Currently most leases are written so that they are operating leases and thus do not appear on the balance sheet. A simplification of the rules in the direction indicated would lead to improved accounting information. It would eliminate the highly subjective elements such as determining bargain purchase, economic life, fair value, residual value, and the discount rates to be used in determining whether or not a lease is a capital lease.

Lessors and Lessees

One objective of FAS 13 was to cause the lessors and lessees associated with a specific lease to treat a transaction in a comparable manner. If the lessor were to show a receivable, the lessee would show a liability. Because of the likelihood that the conditions of FAS 13 will be applied differently, given their highly subjective nature, this comparability has not occurred.

If all leases in excess of one year were recorded as liabilities by the lessee and as receivables by the lessor, there would be increased comparability as to the recording of the liability by the lessee and the receivable by the lessor.

Conclusions

FAS 13 came into being because lessees were not recording the liability associated with the acquisition of an asset (or more exactly the acquisition of the service potential of an asset). If the lease is essentially a purchase of the entire asset and acquiring its use over its entire life, then the lease must be shown as a liability under FAS 13 (for the exact conditions see the four conditions at the beginning of the chapter). But if the lease is for a smaller percentage of life, say, 50 percent, and if none of the other three conditions is satisfied, then the lease is not recorded. This distinction between capital and operating leases is based on highly subjective measures and gives rise to game playing by the several parties. The objective frequently is to write the contract so as to keep the lease off the balance sheet. There is need for a tightening of the requirements for omitting from a balance sheet an obligation to make lease payments. When an obligation to make payments exists, the obligation should be recorded.

Exercises

1. The BC Company has signed a four-year lease for $126,187 per year. For accounting purposes the lease is a capital lease. The firm's borrowing rate is .10.
   a. Record the lease.
   b. Record the expenses after one year. The firm normally uses straight-line depreciation.
   c. Record the comparable expenses if the asset had been purchased at a cost of $400,000.
2. (Continue Exercise 1)
   Record the lease and the expenses after one year if the lease is an operating lease. Compare the expense with an operating lease and with a capital lease.
3. (Continue Exercise 1)
   Define the depreciation of the lease to be equal to the change in value of the asset rather than straight-line depreciation. Assume that the before-tax benefits are $126,187 per year. The tax rate is .46.
   a. Compute the present value of the tax savings associated with the non-debt portion of lease payments. Use .054 as the discount rate.
   b. Compute the after-tax present value of the total benefits throughout the life of the lease.
   c. Show the expenses for each year of use, assuming a .46 tax rate.
4. The XY Company has a cost of borrowing of .10 and a .4 tax rate. It can purchase a piece of equipment for $100,000, or it can lease it for $31,547 per year (first payment one year from now) for four years.
   The financial vice president of the firm wants to show the liability for the lease at $65,588: $(1 - .4) \$31,547B(4, .06) = \$65,588$.
   a. Show the debt amortization schedule for $100,000 debt at a cost of .10 and payments of $31,547 per year.

Time	Amount Owed				
1	100,000				
2					
3					
4					

   b. At what value should the liability be shown? Assume that there is a desire to show the lease liability on a basis comparable to that of other long-term liabilities.
5. Determine whether the following statements are true or false:
   a. If the annual lease payment is less than the annual loan payment (100 percent debt financing), the lease may still be inferior to buy.
   b. Accelerating a lease payment will reduce the after-tax cost to the lessee if the present value of before-tax costs is kept constant.
   c. Deferring a lease payment will increase the after-tax benefits to the lessor if the present value of before-tax payments is kept constant.
   d. If the before-tax lease payments are equal to or greater than the loan payments with the same timing, then buy-borrow will be more desirable than will leasing (assume a positive tax rate). Assume that the

first lease payment is to be made one year from now and that the timing of the first tax deduction is the same as with buy.

6. The ABC Company has signed a lease contract promising to pay $10,000 a year for three years. The payments are at the end of each year. The firm could have purchased the equipment for $24,869 and borrowed funds to finance the purchase at .10. The tax rate is .4. This lease is a capital lease and should be shown as an asset and liability.

   If the company had borrowed the funds, the debt amortization schedule would have been

Time	Amount Owed	Interest	Principal Payment
0	24,869	2,487	7,513
1	17,356	1,736	8,264
2	9,092	909	9,091

Required:

a. What is the *after-tax* present value of the lease payments?

$$B(3, .10) = 2.4869$$
$$B(3, .06) = 2.6730$$

b. If the funds had been borrowed at a cost of .10 (payments of $10,000 a year), what would be the after-tax present value of the debt?

c. What is the present value of the *tax saving* associated with the amount paid in excess of the implicit interest payment of the lease?

7. a. If a series of lease payments has a present value of $5,000,000 before taxes, how will the after-tax present value of that debt be affected by the inclusion of tax considerations; assume that the after-tax discount is $(1 - t)k_i$?

   b. Assume that the after-tax present value of the lease payments for part a is $3,100,000. Record the lease commitment on the books of the lessee.

8. The ABC Company has signed a lease contract promising to pay $10,000 a year for 20 years. The payments are at the end of each year. The firm could have purchased the equipment for $61,446 and borrowed funds to finance the purchase at .10. The tax rate is .4. The lease is a capital lease and should be shown as an asset and liability.

   Required:

   a. What is the *after-tax* present value of the lease payments?

   b. If the funds had been borrowed at a cost of .10 (payments of $10,000 a year), what would be the after-tax present value of the debt?

Solutions

1. a. Asset: Leasehold   400,000
           Liability   400,000
    b. Interest expense   40,000
           Depreciation expense   100,000
               Asset: Leasehold   100,000
               Liability   40,000
           Liability   126,187
               Cash   126,187

c. Interest expense   40,000
Depreciation expense   100,000
     Accumulated depreciation   100,000
     Liability   40,000

If stockholder capital is used no interest expense is accrued.

2.   Lease expense   126,187
     Cash   126,187

The operating lease expense is less than with a capital lease.

Time	Amount Owed	Interest	Principal	Payment
1	400,000	40,000	86,187	126,187
2	313,813	31,381	94,806	126,187
3	219,007	21,901	104,286	126,187
4	114,720	11,472	114,715	126,187

		Present Values in Year			
Time	Cash Flows	0	1	2	3
1	86,187	81,771			
2	94,806	85,339	89,947		
3	104,286	89,064	93,874	98,943	
4	114,715	92,952	97,971	103,262	108,838
		X .46	X .46	X .46	X .46
		160,598	129,624	93,014	50,065
$(1-.46)126,187B(n,.054)$		239,397	184,183	125,988	64,650
		399,995	313,807	219,002	114,715
Change in value		86,188	94,805	104,287	114,715

c.

	Expenses in Year			
	1	2	3	4
Change in value	86,188	94,805	104,287	114,715
Interest	40,000	31,387	21,901	11,472
Total	126,188	126,192	126,188	126,187

4.   a.

Time	Amount Owed	Interest	Principal	(1.06^{-1}) Principal
1	100,000	10,000	21,547	20,327
2	78,453	7,845	23,702	21,095
3	54,751	5,475	26,072	21,891
4	28,679	2,868	28,679	22,716
5	0			
				86,029
				X .4
				34,412

b. $34,412 + $65,588 = $100,000. Liability is $100,000.

5. All are true.

6. a. $(1 - .4)\$10,000(2.6730) = \$16,038$.
    b. $24,869.
    c. $8,831. See the following derivations.

Principal Payment	PV(.06)
7,513	7,088
8,264	7,355
9,091	7,633
	22,076
	X .4
	8,831

or

$$24,869 - 16,038 = 8,831$$

7. a.   Present value of lease is reduced:

$$(1 - t)L \left[\frac{1 - (1 + r)^{-n}}{(1 - t)k_i}\right] = L\left[\frac{1 - (1 + r)^{-n}}{k_i}\right]$$

Present value of debt is unchanged.

b.   Leasehold   3,100,000
     Tax savings   1,900,000
         Lease payable   5,000,000

8. a. $PV = \$10,000\,(.6)(11.4699) = \$68,819$.
    b. $\$10,000B(20, .10) = \$10,000\,(8.5136) = \$85,136$

```
5555555555555555555555555555555555555555555555555555555555555555555555555555555
5555555555555555555555555555555555555555555555555555555555555555555555555555555
5555555555555555555555555555555555    5555555555    555555555555555555555555555555
55555555555555555555555555555555555    5555555555    5555555555555555555555555555
5555555555555555555555555555555555555    555555555    5555555555555555555555555555
555555555555555555555555555555555555555    5555555    5555555555555555555555555555
5555555555555555555555555555555555555555    55555    55555555555555555555555555555
55555555555555555555555555555555555555555    555    555555555555555555555555555555
555555555555555555555555555555555555555555    5    5555555555555555555555555555555
5555555555555555555555555555555555555555555        555555555555555555555555555555
55555555555555555555555555555555555555555555        55555555555555555555555555555
5555555555555555555555555555555555555555555555555555555555555555555555555555555555
5555555555555555555555555555555555555555555555555555555555555555555555555555555555
```

Leveraged Leases

There are at least three parties to a leveraged lease: the lessee, the long-term creditor who furnishes the major portion of the financing, and the lessor who is the equity participant. The lessor furnishes a relatively small percentage of the capital but is considered by the tax authorities to be the owner and thus is able to take the tax deductions associated with the asset (the investment tax credit and accelerated depreciation deductions). Prior to the 1981 Economic Recovery Tax Act, the borrowing by the equity participant using nonrecourse debt was limited by Congress. It was also required that

1. Lessor's equity ⩾ 20 percent.
2. At end of lease, value ⩾ 20 percent of cost.
3. At end of lease, life max ⩾ 20 percent of estimated life or one year.
4. Option price ⩾ value.
5. Lessor must expect to make a profit apart from taxes.

An Accounting Problem

The 1981 Economic Recovery Tax Act relaxed all of these requirements making leveraged leases much more attractive. An accounting problem arises because of the signs of the cash flows' change through time. Because the cash flows go from negative to positive to negative, the "investment" has in sequence a positive net present value, a negative present value, and then a positive present value. At times the investment is more like a loan (positive cash flows followed by negative) than an investment (negative cash flows followed by positive).

The lessor will make an initial investment outlay to acquire the asset that will be leased (this is a negative cash flow). There will then be periods of positive cash flows caused by the investment tax credit and tax-reducing depreciation deductions followed by periods of negative cash flows associated with cash outlays associated with debt repayments as well as increased tax payments arising from the reduced tax shield (the reduced depreciation deductions resulting from the use of accelerated depreciation). Finally, there is a positive cash flow reflecting the residual value of the asset.

It is important to remember that these are cash flows to the stockholders, not basic investment flows.

Multiple Yield Investments

An investment may have more than one internal rate of return (or yield) if there is more than one sign change in the cash flow sequence. A conventional investment has one or more periods of outlays followed by one or more periods of benefits (the cash flows have one sign change). A multiple-yield investment has additional outlays after the benefits have started, so that there is more than one sign change in cash flows.

Consider the following investment:

Time	Cash Flow
0	−100
1	+230
2	−132

The investment has an outlay of $100 at time 0 followed by $230 of benefits at time 1 and then $132 of outlays at time 2. This investment has two rates of return, 10 percent and 20 percent. Figure 5.1 shows the net present values of the investment for different discount rates.

At a zero rate of discount, the investment has a $2 negative net present value, but the investment is acceptable if the firm's time value factor is greater than 10 percent and less than 20 percent. If the required return were 0 percent or 23 percent, the investment would be rejected. Table 5.1 shows that at both 10 percent and 20 percent the investment has zero present values.

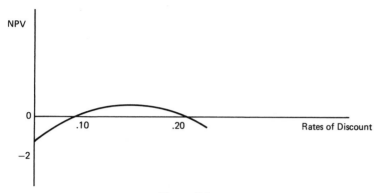

Figure 5.1

TABLE 5.1   Present Values of Investment

Time	Cash Flow	Present Value (.10)	Present Value (.20)
0	-100	-100	-100
1	+230	209.09	191.67
2	-132	-109.09	- 91.67
	Net present value	0	0

If the initial outlay were - $98, the two internal rates of return would be 0 and .34.

Accounting for the Investor

We will assume that the firm has a 10 percent time value factor. The value of the investment and the change in the value for the period (defined to be the depreciation expense) are as follows in Table 5.2.

TABLE 5.2   Change in Value

Time: i	V_i	Value at the Beginning of Period (Using .10)	Period	Change in Value During Period
0	V_0	100		
1	V_1	-120	1	220 decrease
2	V_2	0	2	-120 increase

$$V_0 = \frac{230}{1.10} - \frac{132}{1.10^2} = 100$$

$$V_1 = -\frac{132}{1.10} = -120$$

$$V_2 = 0$$

67

If the change in value of the investment is accepted as a reasonable measure of depreciation expense then the results of operations for the two periods are given in Table 5.3. The return on investment *or* the cost of debt for each period is shown in Table 5.4.

TABLE 5.3 Computation of Income

Time	Cash Flow Revenue (or Outlay)	Change in Value Depreciation	Income or Cost (Revenue less Depreciation)
1	230	220	10
2	-132	-120	-12

TABLE 5.4 Computation of Return on Investment

Time	Investment or Loan Beginning of Period	Income (Net Cost)	Return on Investment (or Cost of Debt)
1	100	10	.10
2	-120	-12	.10

The process involves an initial investment of $100 that earns during the first time period 10 percent or $10 on an investment of $100. In addition to the $110 return there is an additional $120 of cash flow or a total of $230 from the investment, which causes the investment to go negative; that is, it becomes a loan of $120. The $132 has to be paid at time 2. The loan requires $12 of interest on $120 of principal and a total terminal payment of $132. The payment is made at time 2.

These facts are summarized in Table 5.4. The first period has an income of $10 and the second period has $12 of costs. Initially there is an investment of $100 and then a loan of $120. The investment generates income of $10 and the loan causes interest costs of $12.

The exact amounts of income and interest for each period depend on the time value factor chosen. The calculations assumed a 10 percent time value factor. If 20 percent had been used, the income of the first period would have been $20 and the interest cost on a loan of $110 would have been $22 (a total outlay at time 2 of $132).

The multiple rate of return illustration is typical of a leveraged leasing situation.

Separate Phases

FAS 13 requires the use of the *separate phases* method of accounting. Under this method the income of each period is zero if the investment at the beginning of the period is negative.

Adding all the cash flows we have

$$-100 + 230 - 132 = -2$$

There is -$2 of income to be spread over the years of positive investment:

Time	Cash Flow	Depreciation	Income	Investment
1	230	232	-2	100
2	-132	-132	0	-132

cash flow minus the income. The rate used by trial and error to distribute the income over the years of positive investment. The investment consists of the cost net of the nonrecourse debt.

Accounting for Leveraged Leases

Leveraged leases give rise to the multiple rate of return stock equity investments and the type of accounting problem illustrated. The lessor will supply equity capital and will make an initial investment outlay to acquire the asset that will be leased (this is a negative cash flow). There will then be periods of positive cash flows caused by the investment tax credit and tax-reducing depreciation deductions. These positive cash periods will be followed by periods of negative cash flows associated with cash outlays associated with debt repayments as well as increased tax payments arising from the reduced tax shield (the reduced depreciation deductions resulting from the use of accelerated depreciation). Finally, there is a positive cash flow if the asset has residual value.

Assume that a piece of equipment having a life of six years costing $210,000 can be financed with $150,000 debt costing 10 percent (the debt payments are $34,441 per year). The equipment can be leased to a firm at $40,000 per year. The tax rate is .4 and there is a .11 investment tax credit. We assume zero salvage value to simplify the example.

The cash flows are shown in Table 5.5. Table 5.6 shows the debt amortization.

TABLE 5.5   Computation of Cash Flows

Time	Outlay	Lease Revenue	Tax Depreciation	Interest	Tax	Cash Flow
0	-60,000				-23,100*	-36,900
1		40,000	60,000	15,000	-14,000	19,559†
2		40,000	50,000	13,056	-9,222	14,781
3		40,000	40,000	10,917	-4,367	9,926
4		40,000	30,000	8,565	574	4,985
5		40,000	20,000	5,977	5,609	-50
6		40,000	10,000	3,131	10,748	-5,189

*The 11 percent investment tax credit: $210,000 × .11 = $23,100.
†$40,000 - $34,441 - tax = $5,559 - tax = $19,559, where the $34,441 is the annual debt payment.

TABLE 5.6 Debt Amortization Table

Time	Amount Owed	Interest	Debt Amortization Principal Payment
1	150,000	15,000	19,441
2	130,559	13,056	21,385
3	109,174	10,917	23,524
4	85,650	8,565	25,876
5	59,774	5,977	28,464
6	31,310	3,131	31,310

The $19,559 cash flow of time 1 is computed as follows:

Revenue		40,000
Tax depreciation	60,000	
Interest	15,000	−75,000
Loss		−35,000
Tax rate		× .40
Tax saving		−14,000

Revenue		Tax saving		Debt outlay		
40,000	+	14,000	−	34,441	=	19,559

The sum of the years is $6(1+6)/2 = 21$ and the first year's depreciation is $6/21 \times \$210,000 = \$60,000$. The depreciation of each year is $10,000 less than that of the previous year.

The cash flows shown in Table 5.5 have an interesting pattern. There is an immediate outlay followed by several periods of benefits, followed by two periods of outlays. The capital budgeting enthusiast recognizes this as potentially a multiple-yield investment (this investment can have as many as two internal rates of return).

The positive cash flow of periods 1 to 4 reflect the rental payments received that are tax shielded by the accelerated depreciation taken for tax purposes. The cash flows go negative as the tax depreciation expense becomes small and the debt payments continue. The owner would like to abandon the asset at the end of period 4 (the last year of positive cash flows) but would have to be careful of depreciation expense recapture provisions as well as the loan provisions since the obligation to pay continues. If the loan is a nonrecourse loan, there would be an incentive to abandon (or donate) the equipment if there is no depreciation recapture.

The values of the equipment at different moments of time and the change in value are shown in Table 5.7. The after-tax borrowing rate of .06 is used to accomplish the discounting.

Let us define as an investment a sequence of cash flows that consists of one or more negatives followed by positive cash flows. Loan-type cash flows consist of one or more positives followed by negative cash flows. We will use

70

TABLE 5.7 Computation of Depreciation (Change in Value)

Beginning of Period	Present Value (.06)	Cost	Depreciation
1	40,194	36,900	-3,294 (immediate appreciation)
2	23,047		17,147 (depreciation of period 1)
3	9,649		13,398 (depreciation of period 2)
4	302		9,347 (depreciation of period 3)
5	-4,665		4,967 (depreciation of period 4)
6	-4,895		230 (depreciation of period 5)
	0		-4,895 (depreciation of period 6)

the present value column of Table 5.7 to determine when an investment changes from an investment to a loan. A rate of discount of 6 percent was used to accomplish the time (discounting).

Inspection of Table 5.7 shows that for the first four periods the cash flows have the characteristics of an investment, in times 5 and 6 the cash flows have the characteristics of a loan. The present value of the cash flows is positive until time 5, at which point it goes negative, reflecting the future financial commitments of the lessor.

Column 3 of Table 5.8 shows the incomes throughout the life. The $3,294 of income in time 0 reflects the fortuitous circumstances surrounding the investment (it has a positive present value). The income of time 0 would be zero if an internal rate of return of the investment is used as the rate of discount.

TABLE 5.8 Computation of Return on Investment

Time	(1) Cash Flow	(2) Computation of Depreciation	(3) Income	(4) Beginning Investment	(5) = (3) ÷ (4) Return on Investment
0		-3,294	3,294		—
1	19,559	17,147	2,412	40,194	.06
2	14,781	13,398	1,383	23,047	.06
3	9,926	9,347	579	9,649	.06
4	4,985	4,967	18	302	.06
5	-50	230	-280	-4,665	.06*
6	-5,189	-4,895	-294	-4,895	.06*

*Interest cost.

Until time 5 the incomes are positive, reflecting the "investment" phase of the lease. The incomes then go negative reflecting the loan phase. While the negative incomes of periods 5 and 6 are disconcerting to a person considering undertaking an investment, they are logically consistent with the cash flow pattern that exists.

If the positive cash flows of the early years are assumed to be reinvested to earn 6 percent, the earnings from the reinvestment will eliminate the negative incomes. But considering only this leveraged lease, without incorporating the effects of reinvestment, the incomes should be as shown in column 3 of Table

5.8. The negative incomes occur because the firm is in a debt position in periods 5 and 6.

One factor contributing to the negative cash flows of the later years is the tax effects. Since the firm uses the largest portion of its tax deductions in the early years, it pays relatively high taxes in the later years.

Is there actually a liability at time 5? With a normal depreciable asset, taxes will only arise if there is taxable income and this taxable income has not yet been recognized on the books. Thus with a normal asset, the "deferred tax liability" should not be recorded as a liability unless the revenues of the future are also recognized. With a leveraged lease a net liability will arise if the present value of the lease receipts and the loan are recorded. These lease receipts have a lower after-tax present value because the depreciation tax deduction has been used up. The net present value of the lease receipts reflects the lower after-tax value arising because of the absence of a depreciation tax shield, and the present value of the debt flows causes the present value of the total cash flows to turn negative.

Leveraged Leases: Separate Phases Method

Table 5.9 shows the results of using the separate phases method of accounting if an interest rate of .10 is used. Remember that the income of a period must be zero if the beginning investment is less than zero. In Table 5.9 the total income for the entire life is less than $7,112; thus we know that .10 is too low an interest rate.

The depreciable base of the asset is assumed to be the equity investment minus the investment tax credit. While reasonable, this is not conventional accounting (which is too complex for this example). Table 5.10 shows the computations using .11 for the computation of the incomes. We see that .10 is too low and that .11 is too high. The appropriate rate is between .10 and .11. But both these rates understate the incomes of the profitable years and overstate the incomes when there is effectively debt outstanding and the separate phases method of accounting is used.

TABLE 5.9 Leveraged Leases: Separate Phases Method (interest rate = .10)

Time	Cash Flow	Book Investment	Depreciation	Income (.10)
1	19,559	36,900	15,869	3,690
2	14,781	21,031	12,678	2,103
3	9,926	8,353	9,091	835
4	4,985	-738	4,985	0
5	-50	-5,723	-50	0
6	-5,189	-5,673	-5,189	0
	44,012	-484 left over		6,628 too small
				484
				7,112

Explanation:

1. Choose an interest rate of .10.
2. The initial investment is $36,900 (the equity investment net of the investment tax credit).
3. The income of time is equal to .10 × $36,900.
4. The depreciation of time 1 is equal to $19,556 – $3,690 = $15,869.
5. The beginning investment for time 2 is $36,900 – $15,869 = $21,031.
6. When the investment is negative the income is zero.
7. The depreciation schedule does not cause the book value of the investment to be equal to zero at time 6. Try a second higher interest rate, say, .11.

TABLE 5.10   Separate Phases Method (interest rate = .11)

Time	Cash Flow	Book Investment	Income (.11)	Depreciation
1	19,559	36,900	4,059	15,500
2	14,781	21,400	2,354	12,427
3	9,926	8,973	987	8,939
4	4,985	34	4	4,981
5	–50	–4,947	0	–50
6	–5,189	–4,897	0	–5,189
	44,012	292 undepreciated	7,404 too large	
			–292	
			7,112 target total income	

Cash flow 44,012	–	Investment 36,900	=	Total income 7,112
Income using .11 7,404	–	Excess income 292	=	7,112

Conclusions

A leveraged lease, from the point of view of the lessor, has a sequence of phases. In the example, the lease is initially an investment and becomes a loan after four periods. Acceptance of this economic interpretation of events implies that the incomes will be positive and then negative, reflecting the changing nature of the lessor's position. An investment earns income, but a loan results in interest expense. There is no reason to assume a leveraged lease investment earns income in each year of life. Current practice would have zero or positive incomes and would not show the interest cost of the loan phase.

The proposed logic applies to a wide range of real estate transactions as well as to situations in which there is a large amount of "after costs" as in strip mining. Most important, it is necessary to consider the time value of money in a theoretically correct manner if the accounting measures are going to be consistent with the economic facts of the situation.

Exercises

1. a. Assume that an investment has the following cash flows:

0	1	2	3
-819	1,000	-200	100

If 10 percent is used as a discount rate, the net present value is zero. Complete the following table in a manner that reflects the economic characteristics of the investment. Round off to the nearest dollar.

Time i	Value at Time i	Depreciation for Period i	Cash Flow	Income	ROI or Cost
0	819	—	—	—	—
1			1,000		
2			-200		
3			100		

b. For a leveraged lease, explain why the cash flow of an interim period may be negative.

2. Assume that an investment has the following cash flows:

0	1	2	3
-728	900	-200	100

If 10 percent is used as a discount rate, the net present value is zero. Complete the following table in a manner that reflects the economic characteristics of the investment. Round off to the nearest dollar.

Time i	Value at Time i	Depreciation for Period i	Cash Flow	Income	ROI or Cost
0	728	—	—	—	—
1			900		
2			-200		
3			100		

3. The following facts apply for a leveraged lease:

Cost of airplane:	$1,000,000
Investment tax credit (no minimum life requirement):	.07
Marginal tax rate:	.5

Life: four years
Salvage: zero.
Method of tax depreciation: sum-of-the-years' digits
The lessee will pay $300,000 a year.
Cost of borrowing: .10.
Percentage borrowed: 80 percent.

Debt Amortization Schedule

Amount Owed	Interest	Principal	Total
800,000	80,000	172,374	252,374
627,626	62,763	189,611	252,374
438,015	43,802	208,572	252,374
229,443	22,944	229,430	252,374

Required:

Prepare a cash flow schedule for the four years for the owners (the lessors). You can round to thousands.

Time	Cash Flow
0	
1	
2	
3	
4	

4. An investment has the following cash flows:

0	1	2
-400	1,100	-700

There were two rates of return: 0 and 75 percent.

a. Verify that there are two rates of return.

b. Plot (roughly) the graph of net present values.

Net Present Value

Rates of Discount

c. Is the investment acceptable if the required return is .20? Explain.

Solutions

1. a.

Time i	Value at Time i	Depreciation for Period i	Cash Flow	Income	ROI or Cost
0	819	—	—	—	—
1	-99	918	1,000	82	.10
2	91	-190	- 200	-10	.10
3	0	91	100	9	.10

b. Depreciation and interest decrease through time. The revenues are constant. The loss of the tax shield causes negative cash flows.

2.

Time	Value	Depreciation	Cash Flow	Income	ROI
0	728				
1	-99	827	900	73	.10
2	91	190	-200	-10	.10
3	0	-91	100	9	.10

3.

Time	Cash Flows	Interest	Depreciation	Tax Loss	.5 Tax Loss	Principal	Cash Fl
0	-130,000						-130,00
1	300,000	80,000	400,000	180,000	90,000	172,000	138,00
2	300,000	63,000	300,000	63,000	32,000	190,000	79,00
3	300,000	44,000	200,000	-56,000	-28,000	209,000	19,00
4	300,000	23,000	100,000	-177,000	-89,000	229,000	-41,00

4. a.

$r = 0$	$r = .75$
-400	-400
1,000	629
-700	-229
0	0

b.

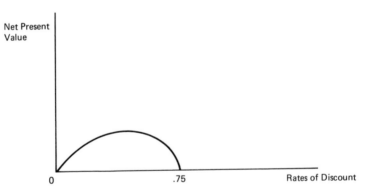

c.

Time	Cash Flows	Present Value (.20)
0	-400	-400
1	1,100	917
2	-700	-486
	Net present value	31

```
66666666666666666666666666666666666666666666666666666666666666666666666666666
66666666666666666666666666666666666666666666666666666666666666666666666666666
6666666666666666666666666666666    6666666666666    666    6666666666666666666666666666
6666666666666666666666666666666666    66666666666    6666    666666666666666666666666666
6666666666666666666666666666666666    666666666    66666    666666666666666666666666666
6666666666666666666666666666666666    6666666    666666    666666666666666666666666666
66666666666666666666666666666666666    66666    6666666    666666666666666666666666666
666666666666666666666666666666666666    666    66666666    666666666666666666666666666
6666666666666666666666666666666666666    6    666666666    666666666666666666666666666
66666666666666666666666666666666666666    6666666666    666666666666666666666666666
66666666666666666666666666666666666666    6666666666    666666666666666666666666666
66666666666666666666666666666666666666666666666666666666666666666666666666666
66666666666666666666666666666666666666666666666666666666666666666666666666666
```

Cancellable Leases
and Inflation Considerations

The lessor (e.g., IBM and Xerox) frequently wants to offer terms under which the asset may be bought and terms under which it may be leased. In this chapter we want to compare buy versus lease alternatives from both the viewpoint of the lessee and the lessor for a cancellable lease. One objective of the calculations is to facilitate the determination of a break-even (indifference) lease payment for the lessor between selling and leasing.

With a noncancellable lease we want to discount all lease flows at a before-tax interest rate to obtain a before-tax debt equivalent and then separate out all nondebt cash flows such as depreciation expense equivalents for application of a different discount rate. The tax saving from the noninterest portion of a lease payment (for a noncancellable lease) is treated in a manner analogous to the tax savings from depreciation expense if the asset is purchased. This complexity does not exist with a cancellable lease. Also, it can be bypassed if the after-tax borrowing rate is used for a noncancellable lease.

We can assume either that the lessor is the manufacturer of the asset being leased or that the lessor buys the asset completely manufactured. The same basic principles apply in either case.

The lessor must not only compute the present values of sell and lease alternatives from its own perspective, but it must also compute the buy versus lease economic analysis from the point of view of the lessee. It is necessary for the lessor to understand the lessee's economic alternatives to do reasonable cash flow planning and to set both the sell and lease terms.

First we analyze cancellable leases where the lease payment is of the same nature as labor and supply costs. It is not necessary to compute a debt equivalent since the lease contract is cancellable. To make the problem realistic, we assume initially that the lease payments increase each year at a rate of j. This can be as assumed to be to the inflation rate, but it can incorporate any special information that leads us to conclude that the specific cost of leasing will increase.

A Cancellable Lease with Inflation

First we assume a cancellable lease with inflation where there are zero taxes. Let

$$j \ = \ \text{inflation rate}$$
$$k \ = \ \text{discount rate before taxes and } r = (1-t)k \text{ is after taxes}$$
$$B(n, i) \ = \ \text{annuity factor for } n \text{ periods and } i \text{ interest factor}$$
$$PV \ = \ \text{present value}$$
$$X \ = \ \text{time 1 cash flow}$$

Let

$$i \ = \ \text{an artificial interest factor defined as}$$
$$1+i \ = (1+k)/(1+j) \text{ or } i = (k-j)/(1+j) \text{ if } k \text{ is greater than } j$$

Then the present value of the lease payments is

$$PV \ = \ \frac{1}{1+j} \ \sum_{t=1}^{n} X \left(\frac{1+j}{1+k}\right)^{t} \ = \ \frac{1}{1+j} \ \sum_{t=1}^{n} X(1+i)^{-t}$$

$$= \ \frac{X}{1+j} \ [B(n, i)]$$

One interpretation of i in the formulation is that it is the real interest rate. For our purposes we need only define it as $(k-j)/(1+j)$ or equivalently as $1 + i = (1+k)/(1+j)$. It is used to simplify the formulation and the calculations.

The formulation $X/(1+j)[B(n, i)]$ gives the present value of the lease stream. It is equal to the present value of an annuity of X (the initial payment) using i as the discount rate, divided by $1 + j$, where j is the expected rate of increase in the lease payments. The factor i captures both the inflation factor and the discount rate.

Example:

Let the initial lease payment be $X = \$100$, the expected price increase per year be $j = .05$, and the firm's discount rate be $k = .20$. We have

t	X_t	Present Value Factors (.20)	Present Values
1	100	.8333	83.33
2	105	.6944	72.92
3	110.25	.5787	63.80
		Present value	220.05

or, equivalently,

$$PV = \frac{X}{1+j} [B(n, i)] = \frac{100}{1.05} (2.3105) = 220.05$$

since

$$1 + i = \frac{1+k}{1+j} = \frac{1.20}{1.05} = 1.1428571 \qquad \text{or} \qquad i = .1428571$$

and

$$B(3, i) = \frac{1 - (1 + i)^{-3}}{i} = \frac{1 - .6699229}{.1428571} = 2.3105$$

The effect on the present value of different inflation rates can be determined readily by varying the values of j and k. We have assumed that i is a constant value of .1428571. While k may be the borrowing rate, there is no reason to restrict its value to one definition in making this calculation.

The calculations would be the same for the lessor and the lessee if they both have the same discount rate and expected inflation rate.

The After-Tax Analysis: A Cancellable Lease

We now want to consider the cancellable lease situation when there is a .46 tax rate. It is necessary to place the discount rate and the cash flows on an after-tax basis.

Now assume a ten-year cancellable lease and an inflation rate of .05. The lease has an initial cost of $583,400. We find it mathematically convenient to compute $X/(1 + j)$.

$$\frac{X}{1+j} = \frac{583,400}{1.05} = 555,619$$

Since the lease payments are cancellable by the lessee, the lease arrangement is more akin to a discretionary cancellable cost than to a contractual debt.

We want to value the lease by placing it on an after-tax basis and use an after tax discount rate. We can use the after-tax discount rate, r, and inflation rate, j, and determine i using the relationship

$$i = \frac{1+r}{1+j} - 1$$

Table 6.1 shows the different lease present values for different values of r for a period of 10 years. The depreciation expense is not included in these calculations since the present value of lease revenues is being computed. The inflation rate is assumed to be 5 percent and the tax rate is 46 percent.

TABLE 6.1 Cancellable Lease with Taxes (present values with $j = .05$, $t = .46$, $n = 10$)

(1) $r = (1 - t)k$	(2) $i = \frac{1+r}{1+j} - 1$	(3) $B(10, i)$	(4) Before Tax $555,619B(10, i)$	(5) = (1 - .46) × Col. (4) After-Tax Present Value
.05	0	10.0000	5,556,000	3,000,000
.10	.048	7.7972	4,332,000	2,339,000
.12	.067	7.1320	3,963,000	2,140,000
.15	.095	6.2788	3,489,000	1,884,000
.18	.123	5.5634	3,091,000	1,669,000
.20	.143	5.1556	2,865,000	1,547,000

If the inflation rate were .15 instead of .05 and $r = .20$, we would have

$$i = \frac{1.20}{1.15} - 1 = .043, \qquad B(10, .043) = 7.991$$

$$\frac{X}{1+j} = \frac{583,400}{1.15} = 507,000$$

The present value of the lease payments with $r = .20$ is now

$$PV = 507,000 \times 7.991 = 4,054,000$$

and the after-tax present value is $(1 - .46)\$4,054,000$ or $\$2,189,000$ instead of $\$1,547,000$. This is the after-tax present value of the lease revenue to the lessor and the present value of the lease payments to the lessee as long as both corporations have the same tax rate, use the same discount rate, and accept .15 as a reasonable estimate of the price changes.

The Lessor's Decision

In deciding on lease terms the lessor must consider the depreciation tax shield. The lessor will be able to depreciate the asset based on the costs of acquisition (we will assume a zero investment tax credit since the investment tax credit can go to either the lessor or lessee and thus is neutral until we know which party receives it).

If the cost of acquisition is $\$2,500,000$ and if the sum-of-the-years' digits depreciation method is used with a life of ten years and a discount rate of .10 we have[1]

$$2,500,000 \times .46 \times .700988 = 806,000$$

The .700988 is the present value of the sum-of-the-years' digits depreciation expense for $1 of assets and a life of ten years.

With $r = .10$ and $j = .05$, we find the present value of the lease revenue to be $\$2,339,000$ (see Table 6.1). Adding the $\$806,000$ of tax shield to this amount, we obtain the value of leasing to the lessor of $\$3,145,000$, which is larger than the cost of $\$2,500,000$. The $\$806,000$ could also have been subtracted from the cost to obtain a net cost of purchasing the asset. This amount would then be compared with the $\$2,339,000$ after tax present value of lease revenues.

Any residual value would add to the value measure. The amount of residual value would have to be placed after taxes and be discounted back to the present.

Selling the Asset

Assume that the lessor with a discount rate of .10 and an inflation rate of .05 is thinking of selling the asset for $\$3,200,000$. The tax basis of the asset is $\$2,500,000$. Assuming the gain is taxed as ordinary income the tax on the sale would be

$$.46(3,200,000 - 2,500,000) = 322,000$$

---

[1] The present value of the depreciation using sum-of-the-years' digits is obtained from H. Bierman, Jr. and S. Smidt, *The Capital Budgeting Decision*, 5th ed. (New York: Macmillan, 1980), Table C, p. 518.

and the lessor would net out

$$3,200,000 - 322,000 = 2,878,000$$

Previously we obtained an after-tax value of $3,145,000 when the initial lease payment was $583,400. Leasing has a larger present value ($3,145,000) than does selling outright ($2,878,000); in addition the lessor keeps the residual value. To make the two alternatives more equivalent, the selling price would have to be raised.

If the firm used an after-tax discount rate of .13 with an inflation rate of .05 the value of i would be .076.

$$\frac{1.13}{1.05} - 1 = .076 \quad \text{and} \quad B(10, .076) = 6.827$$

The depreciation tax shield is now

$$2,500,000 \times .46 \times .639686 = 736,000$$

and the after tax present value of the lease payments is

$$555,619(1 - .46)6.827 = 2,048,000$$

Including the value of the depreciation tax shield, the total value to the lessor of leasing is

$$2,048,000 + 736,000 = 2,787,000$$

Since the present value of selling is $2,878,000, we conclude that the firm would sell with an interest rate equal to .13, but there is close to indifference.

We will shift to an analysis of the lessee's position, where the lessee has a discount rate of .10 equal to its after tax borrowing rate. With $r = .10$ and $j = .05$, the acquirer of the asset has computed the after-tax present value of the lease payments to be $2,339,000 (see Table 6.1). The asset can be purchased at a cost of $3,200,000. The $3,200,000 cost of purchase must be reduced by the depreciation tax shield. The depreciation tax shield for the purchaser will differ from the tax shield of the lessor since the tax basis is different. We have

$$3,200,000 \times .46 \times .700988 = 1,032,000$$

and the net cost of purchase using a .10 discount rate is

$$3,200,000 - 1,032,000 = 2,168,000$$

Purchasing is marginally better than leasing ($2,168,000 is less than $2,339,000), and in addition the buyer has the residual value of the asset. Also, if there is an investment tax credit, there is no question that the purchaser receives it when the asset is purchased.

As structured the users of the asset will buy rather than lease. If there is a residual value, this will further enhance the buy option. Changing the rate of discount would require a recomputation of the present values of leasing as well as buying.

If the lessor wants to lease the assets rather than sell them, then either the lease payments must be reduced or the selling price increased. Alternatively, one or more of the assumptions must change.

Different Estimates of Life

We have assumed that the life of the asset is ten years and that the duration of the cancellable lease is ten years. One might also compute the effect of shortening the life of the lease on the profitability of leasing. Shortening the life of the lease will tend to enhance outright sale since the present value of the lease revenues will be decreased unless the annual lease payments are increased.

If instead of $n = 10$ we were to use $n = 7$, we obtain Table 6.2 The depreciation expense is not included in the calculations since we are computing the present value of the cost of leasing to the lessee. Figure 6.1 shows leasing and buying costs for two different estimated lives for leasing. At $r = .10$ leasing now costs $419,000 less than buying. If the life is expected to be ten years, leasing costs $171,000 more than buying.

Figure 6.1 compares the costs of leasing and buying, but there is a complication since the buy analysis is for a ten-year period and one of the lease analyses is for a seven-year period. One solution is merely to note the qualitative gains associated with owning the equipment beyond year 7 rather than conjecturing the economic efficiencies and costs to be gained or incurred in years after year 7. The residual value at time 7 can be used to reduce the cost of buying if buying is to be compared with a seven-year lease.

A cancellable lease offers the opportunity to switch easily to more efficient and more improved equipment. Buying is a front loading of costs that makes it difficult to switch to improved equipment since the economic capital costs of continuing to use the present equipment are likely to be close to zero. Also, a bookkeeping loss tends to reduce the ease of switching equipment if it is bought and if the performance of management is being closely monitored.

TABLE 6.2 Cancellable Lease with Taxes (present value with $j = .05$, $t = .46$, $n = 7$)

(1)	(2)	(3)	(4) Before Taxes	(5) = (1 - .46) × Col. (4) After-Tax
r	i	B(7, i)	555,629B(7, i)	Present Value
.05	0	7.000	3,889,000	2,100,000
.10	.048	5.828	3,238,000	1,749,000
.12	.067	5.446	3,026,000	1,634,000
.15	.095	4.950	2,750,000	1,485,000
.20	.143	4.249	2,361,000	1,275,000

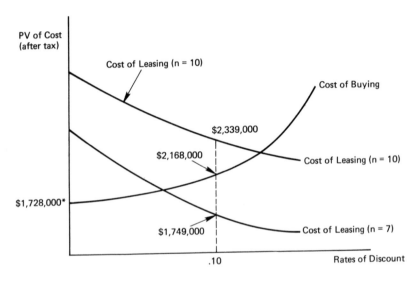

Figure 6.1   A Cancellable Lease: The Lessee

*Equal to $3,200,000 - .46($3,200,000) = $3,200,000 - $1,472,000 = $1,728,000.

A Noncancellable Lease with Inflation: The Lessee

Assume that $n = 10$ and $j = .05$ and that the before-tax marginal borrowing rate, k, is .155. The tax rate is .46. The first lease payment is again $583,400. The present value of the ten lease payments (before taxes) is $3,414,000 using a .155 interest rate. Table 6.3 shows the tax savings resulting from that portion of the lease payments not related to the implicit interest payments. The lease has a .05-per-year payment escalation clause. The lease is not cancellable.

We want to separate the debt type of flows from the nondebt flows.

TABLE 6.3 Debt Amortization ($n = 10, j = .05, k = .155, t = .46$)

Time	Present Value (.155) Beginning of Period	Interest	Total Payment	Principal	.46 (Principal)
1	3,414,000	529,000	583,000	54,000	25,000
2	3,360,000	521,000	613,000	92,000	42,000
3	3,268,000	507,000	643,000	136,000	63,000
4	3,132,000	485,000	675,000	190,000	87,000
5	2,942,000	456,000	709,000	253,000	116,000
6	2,689,000	417,000	745,000	328,000	151,000
7	2,361,000	366,000	782,000	416,000	191,000
8	1,945,000	301,000	821,000	520,000	239,000
9	1,425,000	221,000	862,000	641,000	295,000
10	784,000	122,000	905,000	784,000	261,000
			Using .155, present value		576,000

Discounting the principal tax savings by a zero discount rate, we have

Present value of lease (before taxes)	3,414,000
Less: .46(3,414,000)	−1,570,000
Net cost to lessee	1,844,000

Note that the present value of the lease is $3,414,000 is not changed by the assumption that the tax savings should be discounted at a zero discount rate. The present value of the lease is computed using the before-tax borrowing rate of .155.

The net cost of leasing goes up if we use a higher rate of discount since the before-tax present value of the tax savings is computed using .155, the marginal borrowing rate, and the tax savings are discounted using the adjusted rate of discount. For example, using a .155 to discount the principal tax savings, we have

Present value of lease (before taxes)	3,414,000
Less: Present value of tax savings	576,000
Net cost to lessee	2,838,000

Assume that the lessor is planning on selling the asset for $3,895,000. The lessee calculates the present value of depreciation tax deductions using .155 and finds that it is .59 per dollar of investment. The net cost of buying is

$$\text{Net cost of buying} = 3,895,000 - 3,895,000(.59)(.46)$$
$$= 2,839,000$$

With these facts, the lessee is indifferent. If the lessee discounted the depreciation tax shield at a lower rate of interest (say, the after-tax borrowing rate), the net cost of buying would be decreased (the present value of the tax savings would be increased). But the net cost of leasing would also be decreased (the present value of the tax savings from the nondebt-related deductions would be increased).

The Lessor

Let us consider the same facts from the point of view of the lessor if the cost of the asset to the lessor is $2,000,000.

The net value after tax to the lessor of selling the asset outright is

$$3,895,000 - (3,895,000 - 2,000,000).46 = 3,023,000$$

or

$$3,895,000(1 - .46) + 2,000,000(.46) = 2,103,000 + 920,000 = 3,023,000$$

The after-tax present value of leasing is

$$PV = \frac{(1 - t)X}{1 + j} \ [B(n, i)]$$

where $i = (r - j)/(1 + j)$.

In the example, $r = (1 - t)k = .54(.155) = .0837$, $i = (.0837 - .05)/1.05 = .032$, and $B(10, .032) = 11.57$, and we have

$$PV = .54(555,619)(11.57) = 3,471,000$$

where $555,619 is equal to $583,400/1.05, $583,400 being the cost of the first period.

In addition the lessor will compute the present value of the depreciation tax deductions. If .08 is used as the discount rate for the depreciation tax deductions, we have

$$2,000,000(.46).7477 = 688,000$$

The total value of leasing to the lessor is

$$3,471,000 + 688,000 = 4,159,000$$

Leasing is more desirable to the lessor than selling outright with the terms as described. In this example the lease revenue stream was placed after taxes and was discounted using the after-tax borrowing rate .0837. The discounting was accomplished using $i = .032$. If the lease revenue stream is viewed as being of considerable risk, the lease present value would be reduced by some type of risk adjustment such as using a larger discount rate.

Residual Value Insurance

One of the major risks facing a lessor is the residual value of the item being leased. If the lease is noncancellable, the lessee has a good credit rating, and the financing is defined, the only significant uncertainty is the residual value of the equipment at the termination of the lease.

One solution to the residual value problem is to buy insurance where a terminal value is guaranteed by the insurance company. For example, assume that the lease is a three-year noncancellable lease. Assume that a positive terminal value is required at time 3 for the lessor to break even. If the lessor buys terminal value insurance, the amount of residual value required to break even will increase because of the insurance premium paid. For different residual values we can determine the maximum amounts that can be paid for the insurance.

Example:

Assume that an asset costs $90,000, straight-line depreciation and a three-year life is used for taxes, the tax rate is .46, the borrowing rate is .14, and the lease payments are $25,000 per year for three years. The lessor uses $.14(1 - .46)$ or .0756 as the discount rate.

$$(1.0756)^{-3} = .8036, \qquad B(3, .0756) = 2.5977$$

Assuming a residual value of R, how much could the firm pay for insurance, K, guaranteeing that amount of residual value? The value of K is a break-even amount.

Cost	Tax saving (depreciation)	Insurance cost	After-tax lease payments (PV)	Residual value (PV)
90,000 -	30,000 (2.5977) .46 +	.54K	= (1 - .46)(25,000)(2.5977) +	R (.8036)

$$K = \frac{.8036R - 19,083}{.54}$$

Assume that the value of R that is forecasted is $40,000; then

$$K = \frac{.8036(40,000) - 19,083}{.54} = 24,187$$

The lessor could insure earning .0756 by paying $24,187 for insurance guaranteeing a residual value of $40,000. If the insurance costs less than $24,187, the lessor will earn more than .0756.

If the actual terminal value at time 3 is larger than $40,000, the lessor will regret having purchased the insurance but will be pleased with the lease arrangements just completed. Assuming that $24,187 is paid for the insurance, if the terminal value is less than $40,000 - (1 - .46)$24,287(1.0756)^3 or $40,000 - $16,253 = $23,747, the lessor will be pleased that the insurance was purchased. The calculations assume that the $40,000 is an after-tax value and that the $24,187 of insurance is tax deductible.

Conclusions

The lessor must compute the present values of sell versus lease alternatives from its own point of view as well as the buy versus lease from the lessee's perspective. For cash planning purposes, it is necessary for the lessor to know whether the buy or lease alternative is apt to dominate. If the customers were to shift from buying to leasing, there would be a relative cash drain in the early years. In like manner, if more firms were to shift to purchase, it would result in a greater cash inflow in early years.

The complexities of noncancellable leases arise because they are similar to debt and yet there is a temptation to treat them differently from debt. It is interesting that the stream is like certain debt from the point of view of the lessee but that the lessor is more apt to view the lease stream as being risky, analogous to other risky investments (though somewhat less risky).

Exercises

1. Assume a cancellable two-year lease and zero taxes. The initial lease payment (end of year 1) is $10,000. The inflation rate is .08 (the lease is expected to increase by .08). Funds can be borrowed at a cost of .134.
   a. Compute the present value of the lease payments using the borrowing rate of .134.
   b. Compute the present value using the relationship

$$PV = \frac{X}{1+j} \ [B(n, i)] \qquad \text{(see text)}$$

   c. Now assume a 30-year lease. What is the present value? Which method of calculation did you use?
2. (Continue Exercise 1)
   Now assume a tax rate of .46. The lease term is two years.
   a. What is the after-tax borrowing rate?
   b. What is the after-tax present value of the lease payments?
   c. What is the value of i where $i = (1 + r)/(1 + j) - 1$?
   d. What is the after-tax present value of the lease if the lease term is 30 years?

3. Assume that the asset of Exercise 2 costs the lessor $10,000. The lessor uses straight-line depreciation.
   a. What is the present value of the depreciation expense tax savings? Use a discount rate of .072.
   b. Using the situation of Exercise 2a and the above, what is the present value of the benefits?
   c. If the residual value (after taxes) is $1,200, what is the effect of this consideration on the answer given in part b?

4. (Continue Exercise 3)
   The asset costing $10,000 could be sold now for $18,000. The .46 tax rate still applies. The residual value is $1,200 at time 2.
   a. Should the lessor prefer to sell or to lease?
   b. At what selling price would the lessor be indifferent to leasing?

5. Assume a noncancellable lease consisting of five payments of $20,776 each. The firm can borrow at a before-tax interest rate of .11. The tax rate is .46.
   a. Compute the present value of the lease (debt equivalent).
   b. Prepare a debt amortization table.
   c. Compute the nondebt-related tax savings for each year.
   d. Compute the present value of the tax saving using .05, .10, and .20.
   e. Compute the net cost of leasing if .05, .10, and .20 are used to evaluate the tax savings.

Solutions

1. a. $10,000 \times (1.134)^{-1} = 8,818$
      $10,800 \times (1.134)^{-2} = \underline{8,398}$

      $\phantom{10,000 \times (1.134)^{-1} = }17,216$

   b.
   $$PV = \frac{10,000}{1.08} [B(2, .05)] = \frac{10,000}{1.08} (1,85941) = 17,217$$

   $$i = \frac{k-j}{1+j} = \frac{.134-.08}{1.08} = \frac{.054}{1.08} = .05$$

   c.
   $$PV = \frac{10,000}{1.08} [B(30, .05)] = \frac{10,000}{1.08} (15.37245) = 142,338$$

2. a. $r = (1 - .46)(.134) = .07236$
   b. $(1 - .46)10,000 \times (1.07236)^{-1} = 5,036$
      $(1 - .46)10,800 \times (1.07236)^{-2} = \underline{5,071}$

      $\phantom{(1-.46)10,000 \times (1.07236)^{-1} = }10,107$

   or

   $$PV = \frac{X}{1+j} [B(n, i)](1 - t)$$

   $$i = \frac{1+r}{1+j} - 1 = \frac{1.07236}{1.08} - 1 = -.007074$$

   $$B(2, -.007074) = \frac{1 - (.9929259)^{-2}}{-.007074} = \frac{-.0142998}{-.007074} = 2.0214588$$

$$PV = \frac{10{,}000}{1.08}(2.0214588)(.54) = 10{,}107$$

c. $i = -.007074$

d.
$$B(30, -.007074) = \frac{1 - (.9929259)^{-30}}{-.007074}$$

$$= \frac{.2373465}{.007074} = 33.55195$$

$$PV = \frac{X}{1+j}[B(n, i)](1-t)$$

$$= \frac{10{,}000}{1.08}(33.55195)(.54) = 167{,}760$$

3. a. $5{,}000(1.072)^{-1}$ $= 4{,}664$
    $5{,}000(1.072)^{-2}$ $= 4{,}351$

                                      $9{,}015$
                                     $\times\ .46$

Present value of tax savings $= 4{,}147$
  b. $10{,}107 + 4{,}147 = 14{,}254$
  c. $\dfrac{1{,}200}{(1.072)^2} = 1{,}044$

    $14{,}254 + 1{,}044 = 15{,}298$ (new present value)

4. a.

Revenue	18,000
Less: Cost	10,000
Income	8,000
Less: Tax	3,680
Net	4,320

Cash flow $= 18{,}000 - 3{,}680 = 14{,}320$

The present value of leasing is \$15,298.
Leasing is preferred by the lessor. However, the lease is cancellable.
There is risk.

  b.

$P - $ tax	$=$	15,298
Tax	$=$	$.46(P - 10{,}000)$
$P - .46(P - 10{,}000)$	$=$	15,298
$.54\,P$	$=$	10,698
P	$=$	19,811

With a price of \$19,811, the tax is $.46(\$19{,}811 - \$10{,}000) = \$4{,}513$
and the lessor nets \$15,298. This is the present value of leasing.

5.   Debt Amortization Table

Time	Beginning of Period	Interest	Total Payment	Principal	Tax Savings .46 Principal
1	76,786	8,446	20,776	12,330	5,672
2	64,456	7,090	20,776	13,686	6,296
3	50,770	5,585	20,776	15,191	6,988
4	35,579	3,914	20,776	16,862	7,756
5	18,717	2,059	20,776	18,717	8,610

Net Cost of Leasing

Discount Rate	Debt Equivalent of Lease (Before Taxes)	Present Value of Tax Savings	Net Cost of Leasing
.05	77,000	30,000	47,000
.10	77,000	26,000	51,000
.20	77,000	20,000	57,000

```
77777777777777777777777777777777777777777777777777777777777777777777777777777777777777
77777777777777777777777777777777777777777777777777777777777777777777777777777777777777
777777777777777777777777777    7777777777777   777    777     7777777777777777777777777
777777777777777777777777777    7777777777777   7777   777     7777777777777777777777777
777777777777777777777777777     777777777    77777   777     7777777777777777777777777
7777777777777777777777777777    7777777   77777   777     7777777777777777777777777
77777777777777777777777777777    77777   7777777   777     7777777777777777777777777
777777777777777777777777777777    777   7777777   777     7777777777777777777777777
7777777777777777777777777777777    7   777777777   777     7777777777777777777777777
77777777777777777777777777777777      777777777   777     7777777777777777777777777
777777777777777777777777777777777    7777777777   777    7777777777777777777777777
77777777777777777777777777777777777777777777777777777777777777777777777777777777777777
77777777777777777777777777777777777777777777777777777777777777777777777777777777777777
```

Pros and Cons of Leasing

So far we have considered the economic analysis of the buy-lease decision. In this chapter we review the qualitative pros and cons of leasing. We shall see that there are valid reasons for leasing assets, just as there are valid reasons for buying.

Financing

Leasing is a method of 100 percent debt financing. A lease is frequently easy to obtain and the asset is quickly available. Since leasing is debt financing, it should be recognized that some of a firm's debt capacity has been utilized when a lease is signed. The signing of a lease reduces somewhat the lessee's ability to issue more debt in the future.

While some lease contracts are standard and merely require two sets of signatures, other lease contracts are specific to a given situation and are thicker than *Webster's* unabridged dictionary.

Flexibility

A short-term lease or a cancellable lease offers flexibility. If technology changes, only a phone call is needed to change to the more advanced equipment. There may be no loss to the lessee on the switch.

The disadvantage of the short-term lease is that the lease terms might be adjusted upward by the lessor at the end of the lease term. The lessee has no protection against an upward price spiral. While there is less risk of being stuck with a bad asset, the lessee has given up the chance of having a large residual value at the end of the lease contract. The lessor gains that value.

Flexibility is probably one of the two primary reasons why firms lease. A lease reduces one type of risk exposure.

Bankruptcy

With straight debt it is clear that failure to pay opens up the possibility of bankruptcy. While a lease can be written so that a lessee can walk away from the lease, it is more likely that failure to pay a lease payment will also lead to the same magnitude of bankruptcy risk as straight debt. One should not think that substituting a lease for straight debt eliminates financial risk.

Maintenance Is Cheap and Certain

With leasing the maintenance may be contracted. The certainty of maintenance and the fact that its cost is certain is said to make leasing attractive.

More exactly, these characteristics make maintenance contracts attractive. These contracts can generally be obtained with purchase as well as with leasing. They do not affect the merits of leasing compared with buying but, rather, are a separate decision.

Off-Balance-Sheet Financing

Before FAS 13, leases were largely off-balance-sheet debt and this was thought to be an advantage of leasing. Now capital leases are recorded as liabilities, and in the future we can expect to see the Financial Accounting Standards Board recommend that more leases be classified as capital leases.

Sophisticated analysts are likely to capitalize all leases, independent of the recommendations of the accounting profession. Most experts reconstruct financial statements so that all liabilities are taken into consideration. The artificial distinctions recommended by FAS 13 are not likely to be followed rigorously by a person attempting to use the information to make a decision.

When limits are set by top management on total capital expenditures, there is apt to be an expansion in leasing. The use of leases for this reason is likely to be an expensive manner of conforming to an artificial restraint.

Higher Return on Investment

With an operating lease there is no asset recorded; thus it is easier for management to justify an investment. A higher return on investment is likely to occur because the asset is not recorded. It is somewhat easier to earn a high return on investment if there is little or no investment. All that is required is a positive income.

Just as the off-balance lease does not fool the expert computing the total debt, the use of leasing does not fool the expert computing a return on investment. The asset base should be recorded consistent with the present value of the lease obligation.

A well-managed corporation will control the signing of leases so that leasing is not used as a device to inflate an operating division's return on investment.

Higher Incomes

An operating lease will tend to inflate the incomes of early years of life compared with the expenses resulting from buying the asset. Of course, there might be lower incomes in later years, but management taking a short-run point of view might lease in the hopes of inflating the incomes of the next few years.

Lower Property Taxes

Leasing leads to lower property taxes. This is true, but the lessor pays the taxes and the lessee pays the lessor. There is no reason to see an advantage relative to property taxes unless the lessor is tax exempt.

Income Tax Savings

We have shown that the income tax effects must be computed; they cannot be assumed. All things equal, it is difficult for the normal leasing contract to overcome the tax advantage associated with buying, namely, the use of accelerated depreciation in the calculation of taxable income. Tax rate differentials and interest rate differences can require a modification in the above conclusion.

A Well-Defined Cost

For certain purposes (for example, in the case of a government contract), it is useful to have the well-defined costs offered by a lease contract. Buying an asset requires estimating the asset's life, its salvage value, and its depreciation per year. With leasing, one only has to produce the cancelled check showing the amount paid the lessor.

With buying, there are differences of opinion. With leasing, there are hard facts.

Selling of Leases

This section reviews some of the arguments that have been used in selling leases. You should evaluate the arguments and the comments.

"Defers the expenditure of capital."

A lease contract does not defer the expenditure of capital. It does defer the expenditure of cash and is itself a source of capital. It is debt capital but of a different nature than straight debt. The primary differences are the tax effects.

"The rentals are a fully tax deductible expense."

The depreciation expense and interest expense of buying are also tax deductible. If the tax deductions of leasing are better than for buying, it must be because their present value is larger. This is not likely to occur given the possibility of using accelerated depreciation.

"With a tax rate of 50 percent, the actual net cost of each rental dollar will be $0.50 compared with a cost of $1.00 with buying."

The first part of this statement is true, but the second part is not. Do not compare the after-tax cash outlays of leasing with the before-tax cost of buying. The cost of buying must be reduced by the depreciation deductions. In addition, the implicit debt cost of leasing must be considered in a manner consistent with the way that the buy alternative is analyzed.

"A lease is 100 percent financing."

Yes, and so is debt. It is true that one should compute the total cost of bank debt including the effect of any compensating balance associated with the debt.

"A tax timing advantage will result from leasing."

This is very unlikely, given the possibility of accelerated depreciation. The timing advantage is likely to go to the buy alternative.

"The term of payment is frequently longer with leasing than with alternative financing."

All things equal, this would result in reduced payments per year with leasing, but more payments. Whether or not it is true is an empirical question. Whether or not it is an advantage depends on the size and timing of the payments, that is, on the present value of leasing compared with the present value of buying.

"Flexibility."

A lease does offer considerable flexibility. For example, one can lease a car for a day. This is a real advantage of leasing. However, the costs may increase through time as successive leases are signed.

"Inflation heightens the value of leasing."

The impact of inflation on a fixed (in dollar amount) stream of obligations is well known. The real value of a future payment is decreased by inflation. However, the same conclusion is true with straight debt. In addition, buying has the added advantage of the residual value's increasing in value.

While inflation will increase the value of leasing, it is apt to increase the value of buying even more. There is no obvious reason why inflation should shift the scale in favor of leasing.

"Profits are earned on saved capital."

If lease payments are $20,000 before taxes and $10,000 after taxes and if an asset costs $110,000, there is $100,000 of cash saved. If cash earns .15, the extra earnings for year 1 are $15,000.

This calculation compares apples and oranges. It depends heavily on the comparison of leasing with the use of equity capital. If an asset is financed with $110,000 of debt-paying interest of .10 (before taxes), we know that the cash flows of year 1 will be in favor of buying (the after-tax interest outlay is only $5,500 versus $10,000 with the lease and there are the tax savings of depreciation deductions).

"Leasing offers larger cash flows."

This is not likely to be true in the early years if leasing is compared with buying and using debt. Again we need the present values.

"Borrowing capacity is not reduced by leasing."

This implies a myopic vision on the part of analysts. A lease is a legal promise to pay and this is debt, no matter what the accountants decide.

"Leasing offers obsolescence protection."

A short-term lease does offer obsolescence protection, but at a cost of losing the inflation protection mentioned earlier. A short-term lease opens the possibility of increased lease payments. A long-term lease does not offer obsolescence protection.

"Leasing bypasses budget ceilings."

Spending ceilings should be defined so as to include lease contracts. If they do not limit lease arrangements, they are not effective and will encourage managers to lease rather than to buy for short term cash spending strategy reasons rather than for economic (present value) reasons.

"Leasing from a tax-exempt entity offers advantages."

A tax-exempt entity that can issue tax-exempt debt and does not pay property taxes is an ideal owner of an asset. Whether the entity should be a lessor or lessee will depend on the tax laws in effect. The loss of the depreciation tax deductions and the investment tax credit is a disadvantage unless these tax reduction assets can be sold.

"Leasing places the tax deductions where they can be used."

If an investment tax credit or depreciation deductions cannot be used by the lessee, leasing enables them to be shifted to a lessor who can use them. This is a substantive advantage of leasing. But one has to be careful about generalizations relative to the advantages of shifting tax depreciation shields. Different tax rates lead both to different values of tax deductions and different time value factors, and generalizations must be made carefully.

Two Decisions

With leasing there are two decisions. First, the firm has to decide whether or not the project is worthwhile. Second, a decision has to be made whether the financing should be done with straight debt or with leasing. We are not concerned with the sequence in which the decisions are made as long as it is recognized that there are two decisions. For example, it might be decided that, if the project were accepted, buying is more desirable than leasing but that it is not desirable to acquire the project.

The financing can influence whether or not the project is desirable. For example, a buy analysis might lead to a reject analysis, but since the lease terms are so favorable, leasing might cause the project to be acceptable. Acceptability implies that the asset passes some type of risk versus time value analysis.

If it is decided that straight debt rather than leasing is desirable, it is still possible that the firm will decide to use common stock or some other type of financing. The buy versus lease decision should be made comparing the lease contract with straight debt financing so that the two alternatives are as comparable as we can make them. But after that decision is made it may still be correct for the firm to reject debt in favor of some other type of financing.

Conclusions

Many reasons are offered as to why a firm should lease. This chapter suggests that not all the reasons offered are valid. Several, however, are very important for leasing to be mutually beneficial for the lessor and the lessee.

First, if the lessor is a high tax entity and lessee is zero tax, they can probably arrange a favorable lease (the lessor and the lessee share the advantage of being able to reduce federal income taxes). The shifting of tax deductions such as the investment tax credit and depreciation deductions to a taxpayer who can use the deduction gives value to leasing. Second, leasing can give the lessee flexibility. It allows a firm to buy a small percentage of the life of an asset. Third, leasing is a method of 100 percent financing, and in a period of tight money it might be the only source available.

There are several other reasons why a lease may cost less than buying:

1. The lessor may have made incorrect calculations.
2. The lessor may have economies of scale in purchasing (price discrimination in favor of large buyers).
3. The lessor may have lower borrowing costs than the lessee.
4. The lessor may have different estimates of life, cost of capital, or salvage than the lessee.
5. Different tax and borrowing rate situations may exist.
6. A difference of opinion of the lessor and the lessee may exist as to the appropriate method of evaluating the lease alternative (or computing a fair and profitable price).

Until the calculations are made, one cannot guess as to whether or not buy-borrow or leasing is to be preferred. Make the calculations.

At a corporate stockholders meeting, the president was asked if the firm owned a company plane. The president said "no." The company leased three. Leasing has its advantages.

Leasing also has its disadvantages. A hospital leased computers at a terrifically favorable price. Right after its check was cashed by the lessor, the lessor went bankrupt. The hospital lost its computers and the cash (or if you wish it only lost the cash, it never had the computers).

Is leasing better than buying? Do the calculations.

Exercises

1. Determine whether the following statements are true or false.

   a. If a $1,000 bond paying k interest is sold to yield k, by a firm with a corporate tax rate of t, and if $(1 - t)k$ is used as the discount rate, the present value of the bond is $1,000.

   b. If the present value of lease payments and buy cash flows are equal with zero taxes, the incorporation of taxes will move the decision toward "buy" if the lease payments are equal and at the end of each period.

   c. If $1 of lease payments is replaced by $(1 + k)^{-t}$ dollars t periods sooner, where k is the before-tax borrowing rate, the economic position of the lessee will be improved.

   d. It is possible for one company to have a promise to pay $100,000 a year recorded as a $1,000,000 liability and a second company having a promise to pay $200,000 a year recorded at the same amount, even though both debts were issued on the same day. Assume that the first company is paying 10 percent interest and the second 20 percent.

2. The ABC Company can purchase equipment with a life of four years at a cost of $100,000. The tax rate is .4. It can borrow funds at .05 and repay the loan in four years at a rate of $28,200 per year. With this arrangement the debt amortization schedule would be

Time	Amount of Debt	Amount of Interest	Tax Saving of Interest
0	100,000	5,000	2,000
1	76,796	3,840	1,536
2	52,435	2,622	1,049
3	26,857	1,343	537

   Using .05 as the discount rate, an analyst has computed the present value of the tax savings associated with the interest, S, and the present value of the depreciation tax savings, D, to be

   $$S = 2,000(.9524) + 1,536(.9070) + 1,049(.8638) + 537(.8227) = 4,646$$

   $$D = \frac{100,000}{4}(.4)(3.54595) = 35,460 \quad \text{(assume straight-line must be used)}$$

   The equipment can be leased at a cost of $27,000 per year.
   The analyst has computed the net cost of buying and leasing to be

   $$\text{Net cost of buying} = 100,000 - 4,646 - 35,460 = 59,894$$
   $$\text{Net cost of leasing} = 27,000(1 - .4)3.54595 = 57,444$$

   Required:
   Should the asset be bought or leased? Explain. Two major corrections should be made to the analysis.

3. The Z Company leases equipment. It has computed its weighted average cost of capital to be .11, and it requires a return equal to that on investments.

   It charges for leased equipment based on cost of equipment and maintenance charges. The contracts are long-term contracts (four years) and the lease payments are to be constant each year.

99

The firm has computed its maintenance cost to be $3,000 in a year and increasing at a rate of 10 percent per year.

Management has requested that you compute an equal payment each year (payment at the end of each year) so that the firm will "earn an .11 return on its investment."

Required:

Prepare a report with a recommendation as to how much should be charged per year for maintenance.

4. a. A lessee is given a choice of paying $11,000 at time 10 and $10,000 at time 9 or $10,909 at time 9 and $10,000 at time 10. The lessee has a .10 borrowing cost (before taxes). The tax rate is .4. What preference should the lessee have? Prove (by calculations).

   b. A lessor is given the same alternative described above (of receiving the cash). What preference should the lessor have?

Solutions

1. All true.
2. Cost of buying = 100,000 − .4(25,000) 3.7171 = 62,829
   Cost of leasing = 27,000(1 − .4) 3.7171 = 60,277
   Therefore lease. Note: B(4, .03) = 3.7171
3.

Time	Costs	Present value (.11)	Lease Receipts	Cash Flow
1	3,000	2,703	3,438	438
2	3,300	2,678	3,438	138
3	3,630	2,654	3,438	−192
4	3,993	2,630	3,438	−555
	13,923	10,665	13,752	

$$R\,[B(4, .11)] = 10,665, \qquad R = \$3,438$$

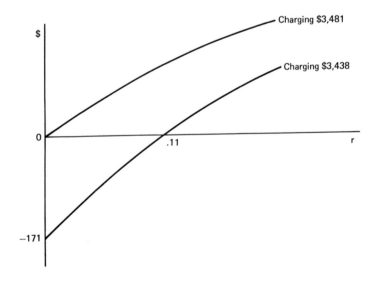

This "investment" is really a loan.

A zero return would result from $13,923/4 = $3,481. This "return" is actually a "cost."

Your report should expand on this theme.

4. a. $1,000 (1 - .4)(1.06)^{-1} = 566$
$909 (1 - .4) = \underline{545}$
$\overline{21}$

Therefore prefer the accelerated payment.

b. Prefer the $11,000 at time 10 and the $10,000 at time 9.

```
888888888888888888888888888888888888888888888888888888888888888888888888888888888888888888
888888888888888888888888888888888888888888888888888888888888888888888888888888888888888888
8888888888888888888888888    8888888888888    888    888    888    8888888888888888888888888
8888888888888888888888888    88888888888      8888   888    888    8888888888888888888888888
88888888888888888888888888    888888888       88888  888    888    8888888888888888888888888
8888888888888888888888888     8888888         888888 888    888    8888888888888888888888888
88888888888888888888888888    88888    8888888  888  888    8888888888888888888888888888
888888888888888888888888888   888     88888888       888    888    8888888888888888888888888
8888888888888888888888888888   8     888888888       888    888    8888888888888888888888888
88888888888888888888888888888        8888888888      888    888    8888888888888888888888888
888888888888888888888888888888       88888888888     888    888    8888888888888888888888888
888888888888888888888888888888888888888888888888888888888888888888888888888888888888888888
888888888888888888888888888888888888888888888888888888888888888888888888888888888888888888
```

The Economic Recovery Tax Act of 1981

The tax act passed in August 1981 drastically changed the nature of a lease as defined by the internal revenue code. We can expect the dollar value of leases in the United States to increase significantly as a result of the changes.

Prior to August 1981 the tax code was very restrictive as to what could be considered a lease and the definitions of lessor and lessee. It was difficult to shift the tax shelters associated with an asset from one entity (a zero tax rate) which could not use them to an entity (high tax) which could use them. The 1981 tax revision opens up the possibility of selling tax credits even though the transaction will be called a lease.

We will consider specific passages from the act to give a flavor of the present situation.

Under paragraph (8) headed "Special Rule for Leases" we have:

(8) Special Rule for Leases
   "(A) In General—In the case of an agreement with respect to qualified leased property, if all of the parties to the agreement characterize such agreement as a lease and elect to have the provisions of this paragraph apply with respect to such agreement, and if the requirements of subparagraph (B) are met, then, for purposes of this subtitle—
      (i) such agreement shall be treated as a lease . . . ."

The first step is to characterize the agreement as a lease since this makes it a lease. The section continues:

"(ii) the lessor shall be treated as the owner of the property and the lessee shall be treated as the lessee of the property."

This section is important since the lessor will be treated as the owner. It does not state that the lessor has to own the asset.

Paragraph (B) defines the requirements necessary for there to be a lease. The most significant economic requirement is that:

"(ii) the minimum investment of the lessor—
"(I) at the time the property is first placed in service under the lease and
"(II) at times during the term of the lease, is not less than 10 percent of the adjusted basis of such property, and
"(iii) the term of the lease (including any extensions) does not exceed the greater of—
"(I) 90 percent of the useful life of such property for purposes of section 167, or
"(II) 150 percent of the present class life of such property."

But more important than the above economic requirement is the next section that indicates there are no other hurdles:

"(C) No Other Factors Taken Into Account.—If the requirements of subparagraphs (A) and (B) are met with respect to any transaction described in subparagraph (A), no other factors shall be taken into account in making a determination as to whether subparagraph (A) (i) or (ii) applies with respect to such transactions."

Consider the requirements that are omitted. The lessee does not have to make payments to the lessor. The lessor may have a bargain purchase at the end of the life. The entire transaction can be designed with its sole purpose being the avoidance of taxes. Paragraph C opens up the possibility of extending leases to a wide range of situations where they were previously prohibited.

The above provisions only apply to qualified leased property. Unfortunately the tax revision is somewhat ambiguous about the definition of qualified lease property. The section reads:

"(D) Qualified Leased Property Defined.—For purposes of subparagraph (A), the term 'qualified leased property' means recovery property (other than a qualified rehabilitated building within the meaning of section 48(g)(1)) which is—
"(i) new section 38 property (as defined in section 48(b)) of the lessor which is leased within 3 months after such property

was placed in service and which, if acquired by the lessee, would have been new section 38 property of the lessee,

"(I) which was new section 38 property of the lessee,

"(II) which was leased within 3 months after such property was placed in service by the lessee, and

"(III) with respect to which the adjusted basis of the lessor does not exceed the adjusted basis of the lessee at the time of the lease, or

"(iii) property which is qualified mass commuting vehicle (as defined in section 103(b)(9)) and which is financed in whole or in part by obligations the interest on which is excludable from income under section 103(a)."

It is clear that new section 38 property (assets eligible for the investment tax credit) qualify. Beyond that we will have to wait for treasury rulings. Finally, section (F) tells how one determines a lessor and lessee:

"(F) Characterization by Parties—For purposes of this paragraph, any determination as to whether a person is a lessor or lessee or property is leased shall be made on the basis of the characterization of such person or property under the agreement described in subparagraph (A)."

Since we have extracted from the actual legislation you should refer to the law for the exact provisions, but the above is a reasonable sample of the new law. It is a drastic change from the past. Now any time two firms have a difference in tax rates they should be able to agree on a lease contract that will benefit both parties.

Previously, the requirement that the lessor must have other than tax avoidance objectives limited the ability of a high tax lessor to acquire tax shields. This limitation has been eliminated.

The Tax Incentive

Appendix I shows that the total value to be captured by the lessor and the lessee because of the lease arrangement is:

Total = Investment Tax Credit plus Depreciation Tax Savings minus
(Present Value of Lease Payments times the tax rate)

If the lease payments are zero, the total advantage of leasing to both parties is equal to Investment Tax Credit plus Depreciation Tax Savings.

Any lease payment (any payment taxable as lease revenue) paid to the lessor tends to reduce the value of the leasing arrangement to the parties of the lease.

With a $1,000,000 of assets which are eligible for the investment tax credit the present value of tax shields are of the magnitude of $400,000 (the exact amount will depend on the life of the asset and the discount rate). Thus the lessor and lessee have a maximum of $400,000 of value to negotiate. If the deal can be arranged so that the lessee makes no lease payments the total value will be maximized.

Under the 1981 Tax Recovery Act it is possible for the lessee to buy and own the asset, and for the lessor to limit its investment to 10 percent of the asset cost. This would make it unnecessary for the lessor to receive lease payments for the lessor to make profits. The lessor could make profits only using the tax deductions (on $1,000,000 the lessor only invests $100,000 and receives $400,000 of tax benefits). The lessee might well require a larger payment than $100,000 by the lessor.

Conclusions

Any corporation buying an asset that qualifies for leasing should evaluate whether or not it can use the tax deductions associated with the asset. If not, it should engage in a leasing arrangement with a firm being taxed which will become the lessor. The two parties should be able to arrive at a contract that benefits both parties.

It is difficult to conject as to the objectives of the legislation described in this chapter. We will assume that the objective is to help a corporation not paying taxes because of losses capture the tax credits it would otherwise lose.

Unfortunately, the present legislation has the loss firm sharing the tax benefits with the lessor. If the objective is as stated it could have been accomplished at a lower cost to the treasury and a higher benefit to the loss firm by a direct investment allowance.

We can expect there to be changes in the future in the legislation affecting leasing. This book was written in as general a fashion as possible so that a reader's understanding was not devastated by changes in the law. The necessity of basic economic analysis of the alternatives will not be changed by an act of Congress.

Appendix I: A Partnership Approach

Let C be the cost of an asset with a tax credit of .1C

    t be the lessor's tax rate

PVD be the present value of the depreciation deductions

    L be the annual lease payments

B(n, r) be the present value of an annuity for n periods and r discount rate.

The value of the lessor if the lessor buys the asset is:

$$V_{Lessor} = -C + .1C + t\,(PVD)\,C + (1 - t)\,LB\,(n, r)$$

The present value of the lease payments to the zero tax lessee is:

$$V_L = -LB\,(n, r)$$

Assuming the lessor and the lessee use the same discount rate, the present value to the two firms in total is the sum of the above two present values or:

$$V = C\,[.1 + t(PVD) - 1] - tLB\,(n, r)$$

With the lessee buying, the present value is -C. The improvement in value resulting from the leasing is:

$$C\,[.1 + t(PVD)] - tLB\,(n, r)$$

Selected References

Baker, C. R., and R. S. Hoyes, *A Guide to Lease Financing* (New York: John Wiley, 1981).

Beechy, T. H., "The Cost of Leasing: Comment and Correction," *The Accounting Review*, 45 (October 1970).

Beechy, T. H., "Quasi-Debt Analysis of Financial Leases," *The Accounting Review*, 44 (April 1969).

Bower, R. S., "Issues in Lease Financing," *Financial Management*, 2 (Winter 1973).

_____ , F. D. Herringer, and J. P. Williamson, "Lease Evaluation," *The Accounting Review*, 41 (April 1966).

Chambers, J., S. Mullick, and P. Weekes, "Lease-Buy Planning Decisions," *Management Science*, 15 (February 1969).

Doenges, C. R., "The Cost of Leasing," *The Engineering Economist*, 17 (Fall 1971).

Elgers, P. T., and J. J. Clark, *The Lease/Buy Decision: A Simplified Guide to Maximizing Financial and Tax Advantages in the 1980's* (New York: Free Press, 1980).

Ferrara, W. L., "Should Investment and Financing Decisions be Separated," *Accounting Review*, 41 (January 1966).

_____ , *The Lease-Purchase Decision: How Some Companies Make It* (New York: *National Association of Accountants*, 1978).

Gordon, M., "A General Solution to the Buy or Lease Decision: A Pedagogical Note," *The Journal of Finance*, 29 (March 1974).

Johnson, R. W., and W. Lewellen, "Analysis of the Lease-or-Buy Decision," *The Journal of Finance*, 27 (September 1972).

Mitchell, G. B., "After Tax Cost of Leasing," *The Accounting Review*, 45 (April 1970).

Myers, S. C., D. A. Dill, and A. J. Bautista, "Valuation of Financial Lease Contracts," *The Journal of Finance*, 31 (June 1976).

Roenfeldt, R. L., and J. S. Osteryoung, "Analysis of Financial Leases," *Financial Management*, 2 (Spring 1973).

Schall, L. D., "Asset Valuation, Firm Investment, and Firm Diversification," *Journal of Business*, 45 (January 1972), 11–28.

_____ , "The Lease-or-Buy and Asset Acquisition Decisions," *Journal of Finance*, 29 (September 1974), 1202–1214.

Vancil, R. F., "Lease or Borrow—New Method of Analysis," *Harvard Business Review*, 39 (September 1961).

Vanderwicken, P., "Powerful Logic of the Leasing Boom," *Fortune*, 87 (November 1973), 132–161.

Wyman, H. E., "Financial Lease Evaluation Under Conditions of Uncertainty," *Accounting Review*, 48 (July 1973).

Index